Crosscurrents / MODERN CRITIQUES

Harry T. Moore, *General Editor*

The Changing Face

Disintegration
of Personality
in the Twentieth-Century
British Novel, 1900–1950

Vida E. Marković

WITH A PREFACE BY

Harry T. Moore

SOUTHERN ILLINOIS UNIVERSITY PRESS
Carbondale and Edwardsville

FEFFER & SIMONS, INC.
London and Amsterdam

To *the memory of my father*

Edo Marković

Copyright © 1970, by Southern Illinois University Press
All rights reserved
Printed in the United States of America
Designed by Andor Braun
Standard Book Number 8093–0410–4
Library of Congress Catalog Card Number 69–1151

Contents

Preface

The Changing Face: Disintegration of Personality in the
Twentieth-Century British Novel *is a stimulating and
valuable critical study by an author whose first language
is not English. Professor Vida E. Marković is a native of
Yugoslavia and Chairman of the English Department at
the University of Belgrade. That she knows English well,
every sentence of her book demonstrates. She has made
various visits to England and the United States; in England she earned her Ph.D. at the University of Leeds
under the direction of Bonamy Dobrée, and in America
she has taught at Princeton University and lectured at
other institutions. She knows many of the novelists and
critics of the English-speaking world.

Before writing the present book, Professor Marković
published two volumes in Yugoslavia on the contemporary English novel. She has written widely for the press of
her native country, and as a journalist attended the Paris
Peace Conference in the summer and fall of 1946, after-
ward flying to New York for the United Nations General
Assembly. She has therefore had a wider experience in
practical affairs than the usual teacher and critic of literature, and indeed her approach to the novel is that of one
who looks at it from the point of view of life rather than
predetermined aesthetic theory. This is implicit in every
line of her book.

The element which most interests her in novels is
character, and in this book she discusses nine characters

vii

prominent in British novels of our time. She is a little doubtful about one inclusion and wonders whether Joyce Cary will be regarded as a major novelist a century from now. But is he thought of as "major" even today? My own guess is that he won't be around at all, like a good many other authors who wrote nineteenth-century novels in the twentieth. Cary's Gulley Jimson is one of the two characters Mrs. Marković deals with who don't altogether disintegrate, and she questions the quality of the optimism that props him up. She also doubts the success of the reintegration of Elizabeth Bowen's Stella Rodney, though she does show that "Stella is hurled down never to recover completely." The defeat of the other characters, including those taken from Joyce, Lawrence, Woolf, and others is never questioned. Beginning with Lord Jim in the very first year of the century, Professor Marković shows how they disintegrate. Her investigation of this problem will be highly useful to modern readers, for she is sound and thorough and always sharply informative.

As Professor Marković explains in her Introduction, she began her reading, as a child, with the great Russian novelists. This was good training. And now she has made an important contribution to the criticism of the recent British novel.

HARRY T. MOORE

Southern Illinois University
May 1, 1969

Author's Note

I spent my childhood in Zagreb, capital of the Croatian province of Yugoslavia. It was there that I went to school and grew into adolescence, and it was there that as a little girl I learned Russian; in the twenties classical Russian culture was being spread by emigres trying to settle down in different countries after the revolution. One day I remember I hid somewhere in the garden with a battered book of stories for children by Dostoevski. This was the first time that I fell under the spell of a character in fiction. It was Netochka Nezvanova who made me shed tears over human destiny, cruel to children of my own age in a far removed country. The echoes of perpetual human suffering had come to me more directly through this Russian book which I was able to read in the original.

The literature that first absorbed me with its reflections of human personality was Russian. Dostoevski, Tolstoy, Gogol, Turgenev were the authors my taste for literature was built on. The interests roused by the little world I lived in, for I was one of nine children, found nourishment in the characters whose destinies I followed in the great Russian novels of the nineteenth century. It is impossible to assess whether this interest in people sent me to novels or whether it was the other way round. One interest supported the other.

An unconscious though close scrutiny of the way human beings behave under different, often extreme circumstances has continued ever since. The vicissitudes and antagonisms in a large, close-knit family were accompanied by the turmoil of public events following closely one upon the other in the interwar period. A darkness began to settle over Europe, cruelly obscuring once firm and unalterable ideas. Yugoslavia itself was laboring under a retrograde provincial regime. My home with its cult of public spirit and respect for human dignity and freedom formed a kind if island of safety and moral security in the seas rising around it.

The restlessness, the growing uncertainty, the clashing creeds of the world at large were elucidated for me by lively discussions at home. At the University of Belgrade the revolutionary movement of my generation blazed up in the latter half of the decade that ended with the outbreak of World War II. Every international event in those turbulent years was taken up by the students, who reacted to the gathering storm in the spirit of the approaching revolution. We seemed to be walking on volcanic ground which might at any time erupt in an earthquake. In all this turmoil my father's figure looms large. Socialist though his inclinations were, he sympathized with the Russian revolution in the manner of Pasternak's Dr. Zhivago; he held firm to his ideas of what was right and what was wrong. Aggression was aggression, from whatever side it came. His friends were being persecuted in Austria, Italy, Germany. A German friend, he told us, had been killed by the Gestapo on the threshold of his home. This announcement cut deep into my mind. I wondered at the time why the gesture that accompanied it and the expression on my father's face so caught my attention. I remember them even now.

About eighteen months later, in December of 1939, I was roused from sleep before six o'clock in the morning. Winter twilight made the shadows in the garden ominous. Several shots fired in quick succession brought me to my father's body. His eyes were not yet completely shut; cold perspiration was piercing through his brow. He too had been shot on the threshold of his home. His words, his gesture, and expression of the year before that now appeared as an intimation of what was to come, seemed a kind of inarticulate explanation of this unexpected and unaccountable murder.

Soon my interest in human personality found more nourishment than my imagination could digest. Acts of heroism were counterbalanced by acts of baseness and cruelty. Some showed supreme courage, some cowardice. Some went out of their way to help, some took advantage and made the most of the misery of others. The grim years of the occupation slowly passed. Terrorism, privation, permanent insecurity were seasoned by periods of imprisonment. Fear worse than the fear of death, fear of one's ability to survive morally under such pressure, alternated with air-raids. All this fused into one long night that ended with the liberation of Belgrade in October of 1944.

Overnight our limited world that had seemed to be separated by endless space even from a neighbouring province opened out through the news flooding into the Yugoslav Telegraph Agency, where my knowledge of languages soon found me. The glorious advance of the Allies ran up against the news of the extermination camps. Remnants of human life reduced beyond reduction, physically, morally, spiritually; heaps of children's shoes, bags of human hair, lampshades of human skin; Jewish women and children gassed or drowned on a raft in the Danube just outside Belgrade, in 1942—all this had somehow to be assimilated by the physically exhausted, morally shaken survivors. Our precarious, ill-acquired balance, attained with some pain, after we thought we had learned the worst—which fortunately had come from the dark, the destructive side—was given the last shock, that of the atomic bombs on Hiroshima and Nagasaki, this time from the other side, the side of the "angels."

An entirely different person from the one hiding in the "rosegarden" with a dilapidated copy of Russian classics turned to the novel again. This time, although I was not aware of it, I was even more desperately in search of human personality. In my quest for some shadow of heroism, like that of the figures celebrated in Yugoslav folk poetry or of the man killed on his threshold, in my desire to find traces of that respect for human dignity which might have served as a barrier against the extermination camps, I looked again to the Russian novel, to Gorki, Aleksei Tolstoy, Sholokhov. But something had been left out of the once great Russian novel —or something had broken in the mind of the once aspiring, optimistic girl.

When the English novel, to which my professional orientation took me, became my hunting ground, it was still the human personality that caught my deepest attention. Everything else seemed fortuitous, accessory. The deeper I went into the problem of the creation of the novel, the more certain I became that it was all about ourselves, that it grew out of the uncertainty as to what we were, the profound distrust, maybe even fear, of what each of us carried in himself. For all those people who had committed the countless atrocities of our time could not have been born criminals. Many of them probably could not withstand the pressure they were exposed to; they had to break under it. If this was so, then were any of us what we thought we were? Had our images of man, our creeds of reason, honor, human dignity, any real value? Had all those who upheld these things at the cost of their lives died in vain? My search continued.

VIDA E. MARKOVIĆ

16 December 1967
Belgrade

Acknowledgments

I should like to express my gratitude to Professor Warner Berthoff of Harvard University, whose expert advice and constant encouragement, especially in the final stages, have helped so much to bring this manuscript to completion, and without whose generous assistance in its preparation it might never have been published. I feel deeply indebted to Professor Richard M. Ludwig of Princeton University for sparing no effort to get the manuscript into print and through whose kind mediation it came into the expert hands of the present editor.

My thanks are also due to Princeton Uiversity for inviting me as a visiting fellow and to Professor Alan S. Downer and the Department of English for making all the resources of the library available to me and surrounding me with an atmosphere in which I could best immerse myself in research in my own field. Last but not least I must acknowledge my debt to the Philological Faculty of the University of Belgrade who generously granted me six months leave of absence, thus making this undertaking possible.

V. E. M.

Introduction

In the course of the last ten years the twentieth century English novel has been the field of my special interest. The present essay comes as a result of long familiarity with it. It is a final assessment of what modern English fiction has meant to me and what I think it can at its best mean to a discerning reader. The approach I have taken is specifically through the image of man recorded in its pages, an image that is elusive and everchanging yet unified and continuous throughout the modern period. For it is through the human figure emerging from it that the novel gains its meaning. Everything else seems contingent. In my conception of the novel every detail must lead to character drawing or derive from it, or else it is superfluous.

The study of these novels and novelists led me to explore a vast amount of critical writing. The mute dialogue that followed revealed that this simple and, to me, axiomatic principle was not universally shared. However much certain critics and scholars penetrated into the mind of the writer, whatever light they threw on the novel in question, they seemed to neglect what appeared crucial to me—the meaning, the value of the leading characters, not as figures in a fiction but as images of man. Sometimes the novelist's fundamental attempt, however slight and uncertain, to find out what we are, who we are, and whither we are bound, was all but left out of consideration.

An increasing certainty that characters in fiction were or should be the most intimate reflection of human personality directed my studies. It made me turn to psychology to find what it had to say about the quality of human personality; it made me consider the transformations characteristic of individual life in this tense century. My attitude to the importance of character in fiction began to form and with it a slightly different, maybe not altogether orthodox view of the novel and of literature itself. The contours of an investigation into the central matter of fictional character and personality began to press on my mind, demanding to be expressed.

There was no study on which I could model my essay. An idea of what the art of fiction really is, what literature in one of its great branches could contribute, began to crystallize. It did not, however, indicate that I could detach character from the work as a whole and get to some ideal image of man behind it. The more I looked into the characters I was dealing with, the more they seemed to appropriate the entire book. Like a stone thrown into a lake they spread their widening circles to engulf the whole of the novel. My early involvement with Russian literature led me again to Tolstoy. I took up *Anna Karenina* to discover that Anna was the book. From the first page, with the quarrel of one couple, the leading movement is unobtrusively introduced. The first marital crisis, superficial as it is, sounds the tragic tones with which Anna will be sent to her doom, carried away by uncontrollable passion for the man she loves. So the answer seemed to be—the character is the novel. But which character, or rather is it just one character? What about Levin? Can a single character invariably be seen as determining the whole? Are there not, in the great Russian novels in particular, more than one character who share the stage and compose the emerging figure of man? The formula, "character is the novel," may hold good, but can any individual character take upon itself the entire novel?

The more I thought about *Anna Karenina*, the less

sure I was of finding a way to prove my initial assumption. But I continued to wonder whether it might not be relevant, with whatever modification, to the English novel between 1900 and 1950, since it was the protracted study of the latter that had confirmed me in that assumption. If modern English novels persistently formed in my mind a distinct image of human character, then there must be some reason for it. There must be some underlying unity in the conception of human personality that, in spite of all evident differences, permitted one to find in modern English fiction a single continuous inquiry into individual human nature, and therefore, too, a continuous moral criticism.

My premise in this essay is that twentieth-century English fiction does indeed compose a connected series of this kind and so constitutes a definable chapter in English literary history. Whatever deviations one may find, whatever radical dissolution or disintegration of individual personality, it is the acceptance of a valid norm or shared moral code—specifically, the moral tenets of the old liberal tradition—that sets the frame in which these deviations, which form the substance of the novels under scrutiny, become discernible. It is the author's moral preoccupation that gives each novel its unity. This might not be so clearly the case for any other modern European [or for American] literature. The uneven, turbulent past of these countries has not led to a single leading moral tradition like the one that has developed in England out of a fully assimilated and diffused national culture. Only a long period of sheltered cultural life in a prosperous community enjoying unchallenged leadership could have produced so optimistic a tradition universally shared, or rather mutely agreed upon, by practically all of its members.

Even if it is assumed that these conditions do exist and that an inquiry based on the principle of the identity of character and novel would be possible, this did not bring me any closer to a method by which I could approach the characters in fiction so that they should reveal themselves to me, yield what I needed, and shed whatever was contingent. But after some consideration the first reaction of despondency gave place to hope. There was no reason why as a common reader I should not be allowed to draw on the whole novel and extract from the maze of words of which it is composed the pattern I was most interested in. My quest appeared the more legitimate since it is through the novelist's hints, details, and allusions that the character forms into a human figure, and the novelist's success ultimately depends on whether the character has come to life in the reader's mind or not.

The minute I decided I could safely embark upon my investigation the question arose: why character in the novel? Why not in the drama, or in the short story? Although I felt that not one of the mediums came as close to the image of man as the novel, I was reassured when I found a confirmation of it in a psychological analysis according to which fiction, in the sense of the "created work of art," both the novel and drama, "draws its life from the 'realistic' world on the one hand and from the world of fantasy on the other." But since fiction, in particular the novel "moves toward reality," while the drama "moves toward fantasy," [1] the characters in the novel can better serve the purpose of this essay. Moreover, characters in a play are created not only by the author's text: the director and also the actors stand between the playwright and the play as produced on the stage, where it comes to life. As for the short story, it does not give the author enough space to develop the characters. Character drawing does not necessarily form its central core. It is therefore only in the novel that the author addresses the reader directly and at sufficient length to offer his full vision of life without mediation. The novel is the narrative art in which the author's attitude to human existence and its values comes to the reader in the most directly identifiable form, presenting a figure like himself, a character trying to build its destiny in the tangle of everyday life.

Since the novel seems to disclose and communicate, more directly and more fully, the sense of life from the point of view of the complete man, we shall try to trace in the characters of the modern English novel the general trend of our own development. Closely attached though they are to the English background and ethos, they are probably broadly relevant to the man of Western civilization and may give some indication as to the fluctuating norm of human behavior in our fluid, drifting age.

The next question is which characters are to be chosen as most appropriate for an examination of this kind. Obviously only those who seem to be fully alive, which means those who develop in the novel and so come closer to life. This rules out purely comic characters and caricatures, all those figures who are static. Characters who serve only to voice the author's ideas, and have no life of their own apart from that function in the novel, like Huxley's, or those that impersonate some devouring passion, like those of Ivy Compton-Burnett, could not assist in this quest. Characters who follow too closely on the trodden path and do not contribute any new insight into the human personality, even if produced by some excellent novelists writing on traditional lines, could not offer anything either. This leaves out Arnold Bennett, Galsworthy, Maugham, J. B. Priestley, Cronin, and some other favorites. Thus the selecton of relevant authors is reduced. The only question still open is that of the characters themselves. We cannot assume that a scientific objectivity is possible, nor do we think it necessary. If we try to detect what the common reader has gleaned from the reading of the English novel of the first half of this century, what has impressed itself on his mind with regard to the changing human figure, we must leave a margin, and a considerable one, for his personal tastes and values.

In the choice of characters from the gallery of portraits each of the novelists has created we can fall back upon the following conception of artistic creation: if the difference between the creative artist and ourselves consists of the former's ability to give free play to his emotions and instincts, and, while fertilizing them with his creative imagination, escape the control of conventional understanding and recreate for us a vision relevant to our experience of life, his most representative figure will be the one least tainted by his compliance with the conventions of the age—the one that arose from his profoundest being, deep below the consciousness which guides him in his daily existence. It will be the kind of creation by which, once accomplished, he is as surprised as the reader, something he discovers not merely in himself, bur rather through himself. This implies that novels with a deliberate thesis would be less likely to supply the relevant figure. The more emancipated the author from whatever bonds he may have, the more lifelike his characters, i.e., the more representative of the changing conception of the human personality we are pursuing in this essay. Of unconscious bonds the novelist is not aware, nor should he be. They prompt him to create this type of human personality and not that, representing this norm of behavior and not that one. Without these internal bonds and ties, who knows how acquired, this subconscious allegiance to some and just as sturdy rejection of others, he could hardly have produced a figure that could serve for this kind of investigation.

The characters finally decided upon were: Conrad's Jim, D. H. Lawrence's Ursula Brangwen, James Joyce's Stephen Dedalus, Virginia Woolf's Clarissa Dalloway, Evelyn Waugh's Tony Last, Graham Greene's Major Scobie, Rosamond Lehmann's Mrs. Jardine, Elizabeth Bowen's Stella Rodney, and Joyce Cary's Gulley Jimson. All these characters seemed to lend themselves to the type of exploration here defined. They were complete in the sense that they resulted from a completed process of artistic realization. They represented their author's full creation of a human figure. They contained the profoundest confession of their author's attitude to life, as open to ourselves as his contemporaries, and yet they were detached enough from their author to exist in their own right in the world of fiction.

When my investigation brought me to James Joyce's Stephen, I realized that I confronted a special case, that Stephen had not been entirely emancipated from his author. With this character James Joyce apparently could not extricate himself from the fiction he had created. He could not make the liberating synthesis. He could not wrench himself from his dreamland and at the same time ensure his imagination free access into the world of fantasy. To explain the figure of Stephen, the figure of his creator would have to be evoked. And was the case of Clarissa Dalloway any different? She, too, it seemed, could not be elucidated without reference to her creator?

The critical issues involved in my treatment of these two cases cannot be fully discussed here. I merely wish to explain that my references to the author's lives are not accidental, nor are they lapses in critical method. They are deliberate digressions which seemed indispensable to developing the crucial points of this book's argument. They are necessitated by the goal to which the rules of this self-imposed game had to be subordinated. What I was trying to do was to trace a process of moral disintegration, as documented, at times even anticipated, by the characters of several novels. To achieve this end I needed the freedom to depart from the critical etiquette which bars consideration of the author's own life. But is the critic altogether responsible for his breach of courtesy? Is it not rather the novelist himself who, in such a case, has invited it? Though the disciplined exercise of craftsmanship and objectification appears to be the reverse of autobiographical writing, the effort to use craftsmanship as an "escape from personality" [T. S. Eliot's phrase] [2] is itself a way of expressing personality and of making a basic statement about human character. James Joyce and Virginia Woolf have, so it appears, allowed their own apprehension of reality, their practice of art, to be submerged by the world of fiction they have created.

With them it was fiction that impinged on reality.

Now that the ground has been cleared, let us try and view the English novel produced in this century as a continuous process and see if we can discern in the *changing face* of its protagonists the various transformations through which its characters have gone. For, if characters in fiction reflect real people, then their changing features are relevant to life, and, if closely watched and analyzed, may yield insight into what has been happening to *man*, to ourselves, in the first half of this century.

The Changing Face

Disintegration of Personality
in the
Twentieth-Century British Novel
1900–1950

1

Jim

The human heart is vast enough to contain all the world. It is valiant enough to bear the burden, but where is the courage that would cast it off? [1]

In Conrad's opinion, the novelist should not only make the reader feel, hear, visualize what is presented to him. He should above all make him *see*. Figures in fiction should be more vivid than people in life, since, as is not the case in real life, the reader is initiated into their lives from the inside. Obsessed with man as a conscious being, with an elevated idea of the function of the novelist who deals with man's consciousness and with affairs of conscience, Conrad is determined to make us *see*. But "seeing," for Conrad, has a more complex meaning than merely the physical sense of sight. Conrad saw man and his destiny as preordained in consciousness, and as always at the mercy of consciousness. Man's destiny is governed by his awareness of whether or not he has lived up to its standards. Such a conception of human personality, Conrad thought, could best be expressed in a novel which deals directly with the breach of this inward code of honor and with its consequences.

While writing *Lord Jim* [1900], Conrad was coming into what may be called his early maturity. He had found a means of expressing directly what was revealed to him in the process of creation. His search into the human mind was still so fresh and new that he exulted in the step-by-step process of discovery it was leading to. Stimulated by what was being disclosed to him, he daringly advanced. His profound concentration releasing him from inhibitions, he freely communicated what he discovered. But he had not come to the stage at which this concentration and the artistic discoveries that followed had become an acquired routine. The process of creation and revelation still involved an exhilaration that was to be shared with the reader. He had learned how to make the novel self-contained—the narrator being entirely within the novel—and how by this means to draw the reader more directly into it. The assumed presence of the reader supplies yet another angle of vision which gives the novel verisimilitude. Conrad was discovering the existence of the dark underside of human personality, but he was not himself drawn into it. He would not allow the "heart of darkness" to mesmerize him, to suck him under, the way an exhausted swimmer is pulled down by the ominous whirlpool he can no longer resist. He kept the figure at the center of his vision clear. And indeed in *Lord Jim* the features of the chief character are not blurred. Jim himself retains as unscathed a front as is needed to impress the reader with the external solidity of individual human personality the more to affect him with the tragedy of human fragility lurking beneath.

According to Conrad's own statement, Jim suffers from "the acute consciousness of lost honour." [2] That is all. Out of this Jim's figure grew, out of this the story evolved, from the author's first vision of him as he saw "his form pass by—appealing—significant—under a cloud—perfectly silent" [3] until the last page when the narrator, Marlow, winds up his story, none the wiser after the long exploration into the young figure that had caught his fancy: "And that's the end. He passes away under a cloud, inscrutable at heart, forgotten, unforgiven, and excessively romantic." [4] Conrad's narrator ends as though in despondent hopelessness as to the secret he has tried to unravel. Yet in the foregoing pages he has discovered more about Jim—who is, the author never tires repeating it, "one of us"—than anybody at that time. He has not sought "fit words for his meaning" [5] in vain.

He was an inch, perhaps two, under six feet, powerfully built, and he advanced straight at you with a slight stoop of the shoulders, head forward, and a fixed from-under stare which made you think of a charging bull. His voice was deep, loud, and his manner displayed a kind of dogged self-assertion which had nothing aggressive in it. It seemed a necessity, and it was directed apparently as much at himself as at anybody else. He was spotlessly neat, apparelled in immaculate white from shoes to hat, and in the various Eastern ports where he got his living as shipchandler's water-clerk he was very popular.[6]

Jim comes from a country parsonage, favorite son of a fond father, one of those parsons who simply accept the teachings of the church and apply it in their life without inquiring into anything. "Virtue is one all over the world," he writes to his son, "and there is only one faith, one conceivable conduct of life, one manner of dying." [7] All the other children seem to have taken the same line in life and joined the masses of people who exist, but do not add anything to push the world a bit forward. "It seems amazing," Marlow muses, "that he should belong to it, he to whom so many things 'had come.' Nothing ever came to them; they would never be taken unawares, and never be called upon to grapple with fate." [8] Jim has that in him that does not allow him to proceed happily along the beaten track. It is the sea with its adventures and dangers that attracts him. And so he chooses the lot that puts him to a test he is not ready to pass.

Throughout his training nothing has happened to disturb the boy's heroic delusions about himself. There was an emergency on the training ship to which he did not respond as a hero but he assumed that it was of no consequence. "He had enlarged his knowledge more than those who had done the work. When all men flinched, then—he felt sure—he alone would know how to deal with the spurious menace of wind and seas." [9] He went to sea after two years training and "entering the regions so well known to his imagination, found them strangely barren of adventure." [10] Only once did he have a glimpse of the earnest anger of the sea, but then he was disabled and not expected to do anything. He was seized by anguish, but once the storm was over he soon forgot about it. He pushed the undesired sensation as far below his consciousness as he could.

So the unexpected emergency on the *Patna*, where he was chief mate, took him unawares. It happened while they were sailing steadily; absolute calm reigned all around:

> At such times his thoughts would be full of valorous deeds: he loved these dreams and the success of his imaginary achievements. They were the best parts of life, its secret truth, its hidden reality. They had a gorgeous virility, the charm of vagueness, they passed before him with a heroic tread; they carried his soul away with them and made it drunk with the divine philtre of an unbounded confidence in itself. There was nothing he could not face.[11]

Then the ship ran into something and broke right through the middle. Water began to pour in. The ship was full of pilgrims going to Mecca. There were seven lifeboats to eight hundred people. There did not seem a straw of a chance of either saving the passengers or avoiding the disaster. Courage failed Jim. He followed the escaping crew, at the head with the skipper, a depraved, uprooted German. At the very last minute, as if acting in a dream, he jumped into the lifeboat and left the ship and its human cargo to its own fate.

But the *Patna* did not sink. The other accused officers, however, managed to escape. Jim is the only one to face trial. He refuses the offer to clear out before the verdict is passed. The verdict of guilty and the cancellation of his certificate leave him destitute. Were it not for the helping hand extended by Marlow, the narrator of the tale, Jim would probably have drifted aimlessly and soon joined the depraved loiterers of Far Eastern ports, lost to themselves and humanity, homeless, declassed. He might have taken to drink, or become a drug addict, and finished in the lowest depths of society. Through Marlow, a kind of humanized Providence, he is given yet another and then another and another chance. He lets them all go. The minute the *Patna* case is mentioned in the port where he serves as waterclerk, he quits. In the end, through the old sage, Stein, one of the important oracles of the story, Jim is given another and the greatest chance, that of beginning his life anew. On a remote island, at Patusan, he creates a new existence. He becomes the country's leader. Everything seems to go well until Captain Brown's pirate ship and his gang of desperadoes come to Patusan. Faced with an outcast like himself, Jim again falters. He loses control of his reason and jeopardizes the security of the community. Cheated by Brown he offers his life in return and unflinchingly takes the punishment.

Jim is a young man of good parentage. He comes from the right place. He is "one of us." [12] And yet the moment all this comes to be tested, he fails. The whole of the book is concerned with the author's attempt to explain Jim, not as a special case, for that would have deprived it of its intrinsic significance, but as "one of us." What is Jim? Marlow watches him closely, irresistibly drawn to him as though by magic. Is it because the "knowledge of his weakness . . . made it a thing of mystery and terror —like a hint of a destructive fate ready for all whose youth—in its day—had resembled his youth?" [13] Or did he feel that what brought Jim to the dock is something from which none of us is free? This is implied by his words: "in what was I better than the rest of us to refuse him my pity?" [14] Where is the answer? Gradually as the "yarn" unfolds, the contours of Jim's ethical being—and this is what the reader is presented with, this is what makes Jim one of the most engrossing characters in modern English fiction—become clearer, not because the author was able to make the walls of Jim's being transparent, but because, while dipping into himself to elucidate his conception, Conrad detected that his own being echoed to that of Jim. It responded to the same vibrations. Not by separating him from mankind and watching him as a being apart, but by treating him as "one of us," identifying himself with him, the author begins to understand him. The answers he formulates are uttered by Marlow. Nothing breaks the emotional continuity: the characters and their shadows, the figure of the protagonist and the commonsense voice of the chorus, are wholly inside the novel. Nothing alien violates its completeness, nothing takes away from Jim's figure. And yet he escapes. It is his elusiveness that probably glues Marlow's eyes to him:

> He was outwardly so typical of that good, stupid kind we like to feel marching right and left of us in life, of the kind that is not disturbed by the vagaries of intelligence and the perversions of—of nerves, let us say. He was the kind of fellow you would, on the strength of his looks, leave in charge of the deck—figuratively and professionally speaking . . . He looked as genuine as a new sovereign, but there was some infernal alloy in his metal.[15]

In spite of the pain he suffers, Marlow watches the inquiry to the end, and things begin to open up to him. He tries to clear them up for himself while spinning the yarn to his friends throughout that long night. "Nothing more awful than to watch a man who has been found out, not in a crime but in a more than criminal weakness," he remarks. "The commonest sort of fortitude [that] prevents us from becoming criminals in a legal sense": [16] that is what failed Jim. But Marlow feels that this is not only Jim's predicament: "it is from weakness unknown, but perhaps suspected, as in some parts of the world you suspect a deadly snake in every bush—from weakness that may lie hidden, watched or unwatched, prayed against or manfully scorned, repressed or maybe ignored more than half a lifetime, not one of us is safe." [17]

This is the first glimpse deep into Jim, and it is gleaned from watching him exposed to the eyes of "men and women by no means clever or amusing, but whose very existence is based upon honest faith, and upon the instinct of courage." [18] Jim lacks the "unthinking and blessed stiffness before the outward and inward terrors, before the might of nature, and the seductive corruption of men . . ." [19] He is vulnerable "to the strength of facts, to the contagion of example, to the solicitation of ideas." [20] It is the influence of ideas that is the hardest to resist. For ideas "are tramps, vagabonds, knocking at the back-door of your mind, each taking a little of your substance, each carrying away some crumb of that belief in a few simple notions you must cling to if you want to live decently and would like to die easy!" [21] Jim's undoing is not a lack of consciousness, the distinguishing attribute of man, but an excess of it. It is his imagination — "Imagination, the enemy of men, the father of all terrors" [22] — that has prevented him from acting on a natural manly impulse. But this is not the answer Conrad himself can accept. The whole book is an attempt to find a further answer to the dilemma of conscious human life. It is a search into the conflict, psychological, ethical and moral, between the inner and the outer reality.

In a long discourse with Jim, Marlow gets a firsthand report of the event. More than that, he gets the boy's instinctive self-vindication. Jim attempts to dissociate himself from the other members of the crew. They are different, they do not belong to the heroic world of illusion to which he, somehow, in spite of his disgrace, still belongs. He had indeed jumped, although he cannot quite remember the event as a deliberate action. In a way it was his vision of the whole disaster that overcame him, the behavior of the senior members of the crew and even more the vision of eight hundred people trying to save their lives in seven boats.

> "Somebody was speaking aloud inside my head," he said a little wildly. "Eight hundred people and seven boats — and no time! Just think of it!" He leaned towards me across the little table, and I tried to avoid his stare. "Do you think I was afraid of death?" he asked in a voice fierce and

low. He brought down his open hand with a bang that made the coffee-cups dance. "I am ready to swear I was not—I was not . . . By God—no!" He hitched himself upright and crossed his arms; his chin fell on his breast.[23]

It is not only Marlow Jim must win over; it is himself he must protect, delude, deceive, or else he is done for. Marlow's role then is not simply to listen, understand, and judge. He is called upon to take part in this major deception played by Jim on himself. "He was not speaking to me, he was only speaking before me, in a dispute with an invisible personality, an antagonistic and inseparable partner of his existence—another possessor of his soul . . . [he] did not want a judge. He wanted an ally, a helper, an accomplice." [24]

Another voice speaking in his ear, repeating stubbornly, eight hundred people and seven boats, during the fatal seconds before he jumped: the devil tempting one directly is no novelty either in folklore or literature. This is what Hamlet is afraid of and why, as he alleges, he does not trust his father's ghost. The root of the matter for Conrad is in the fundamental duplicity of human nature: the dialectical existence of good and evil as elements in one and the same human consciousness. He challenges the age-old dichotomy, good on the one side, evil on the other.

Jim's repeated question of what he should have done extorts Marlow's furious answer: "Sink—curse you! Sink!" [25] The obvious code of behavior of a professional sailor would have dictated to Jim that he sink with the ship, but he had refused to listen to it. Even now, speaking to Marlow, a cry of pain is wrung from him: "Ah! what a chance missed! My God! what a chance missed!" [26] He is overwhelmed by the disgrace. Yet his inability to deal with reality still prevents him from recognizing the guilt which would have been the first step towards his absolution.

Marlow's attempts to get him a job fail one after another because so long as Jim cannot consciously accept his guilt, he must run away from the mention of the

Patna case. Marlow would like to help him to turn a new
page, but Jim cannot do so until he settles his account
with the preceding one. Jim stubbornly refuses to do it.
He cannot accept the simple necessity, the inevitable
fact that "what is done cannot be undone." [27] If you
cannot live with a fact then you yourself must change,
for the fact once accomplished is unalterable. Conrad
knows that "the truth can be wrung out of us only by
some cruel, little, awful catastrophe." [28] Jim has suffered
a catastrophe, yet he cannot yield the truth. Therefore
he is opaque. This does not take away the interest he has
for us, for it is not due to the author's inability to make
him transparent. It is just because Jim is true to life that
we cannot see into him. His fear of self-knowledge makes
him equally opaque to himself and to the reader. He is
not aware of this fear. Nor should we expect him to be,
since, in Marlow's words, "no man ever understands
quite his own artful dodges to escape from the grim
shadow of self-knowledge." [29]

Marlow turns to Stein, one of his oldest friends, a rich
merchant and a well-known figure in those parts. Almost
a scholar, Stein's philosophy springs from his authentic
knowledge of life. He has not dodged the pitfalls set by
destiny. Stein immediately diagnoses Jim's case: "He is
romantic. He wants to be a saint, and he wants to be a
devil—and every time he shuts his eyes he sees himself as
a very fine fellow—so fine as he can never be . . . It is
not good for you to find you cannot make your dream
come true, for the reason that you not strong enough are,
or not clever enough." [30] And then Stein develops his
theory of life, derived from his own eventful and painful
experience:

> "A man that is born falls into a dream like a man who
> falls into the sea. If he tries to climb out into the air as
> inexperenced people endeavour to do, he drowns . . .
> No! I tell you! The way is to the destructive element
> submit yourself, and with the exertions of your hands and
> feet in the water make the deep, deep sea keep you up
> . . . In the destructive element immerse. . . . That was

the way. To follow the dream, and again to follow the dream—and so—*ewig—usque ad finem.*" [31]

In Patusan Jim lives for once in accordance with his ideals. He is convinced that fear can no longer overtake him. He seems to have "at last mastered his fate." [32] He wins "the trust, the fame, the friendship, the love," [33] of the people. He becomes their leader in war and peace, respected as the judge dispensing justice, admired as a legendary hero whose might surpasses that of ordinary mortals. He even wins the love of the only white girl, Jewel, whose guardian stepfather, a monster in human shape, the half-caste Portuguese, Cornelius, dogs Jim's steps determined to get him out, get him killed, if possible, since his existence, based on iniquity, cannot flourish in the new order of justice and prosperity that Jim has ensured for the community.

The past seems to be forgotten, pushed deep into the back of Jim's mind. He seems to have detached himself entirely from the world "out there" for which he was not "good enough." [34] And yet, on visiting him, Marlow, who interprets Jim to the reader, feels that Jim is not completely rooted in the soil of Patusan. He senses that his heroic conduct is inspired by an urge for rehabilitation. All his achievements in Patusan are unconsciously designed to prove to the world and above all to himself —which is the hardest—that he is not a coward. Jim's desperate broken cry to the departing Marlow: "Tell them . . ." and his inability to answer Marlow's question, "Tell who?" [35] shows that the deeply buried wound has never healed. Jim keeps it open, and so it may fester any time.

His wife Jewel does not understand him. She feels that she has not got full hold of Jim. She is afraid that the world he has come from may claim him. She resents the presence of anyone who has come from there, from the "Unknown." Marlow's assurance that Jim will never leave her, or leave Patusan, does not convince her. His explanation that this other world will not claim him because "he is not good enough" [36] leaves her puzzled, incredulous. It hurts her. Jewel is not the only one who does not understand Jim. She feels that he eludes her like a figure in a dream. Nobody can understand him, because he does not understand himself. By barring his own access into himself, he has barred the whole of mankind and so he lives in profound isolation. Jim protests that nothing can frighten him any longer. Marlow, representing the world's opinion, is himself deluded into believing him on the ground that perhaps "nothing could touch him since he had survived the assault of the dark powers." [37]

When the redoubtable Captain Brown asks what has made him come to the island, Jim's assumed security, his proven courage, immediately fail him. Had he fearlessly confronted the past, he would have been able to answer without hesitation; he might even have refused to answer and laughed the question off. Since he lacks this most elementary courage he is taken aback. The experienced rascal whose success in iniquitous exploits, whose very existence, depends on his ability to take stock of his adversary, instinctively sizes Jim up. "He admitted that he couldn't be scared, but there was a way as 'broad as a turnpike, to get in and shake his twopenny soul around and inside out and upside down—by God!' " [38] While talking to Jim, "as if a demon had been whispering advice in his ear" he insinuates: "when 'it came to saving one's life in the dark, one didn't care who else went— three, thirty, three hundred people' " [39]; he subtly refers "to their common blood" and "common experience"; he offers "a sickening suggestion of common guilt, of secret knowledge that was like a bond of their minds and of their hearts." [40] Jim's general appearance of spotless honesty, his idealistic zeal, his trust in the very ideals Brown has furiously rejected, irritate Brown, who now would like to harm Jim even if it does not advance his own interests.

Brown has immersed himself in his destructive element, he exults in his wickedness. He keeps no illusions about himself except one, that he has "trampled all the earth under his feet." [41] Jim is inclined to believe in Brown's fundamental honesty not because he is naïve, *innocent*, but because he wants to believe. Brown stands for Jim's own dark side that he has tried, at fantastic cost, to ignore. Now that it is there, solidly in front of him, he hopes against hope that Brown is not really irredeemable, that the human spark has never died in him and so can be revived. For, if this is proved true, then his own dark side is likewise redeemable. Acting against reason and going against the common sense of the old leaders of the community he obtains a clear road for Brown and his men meanwhile pledging his own life "for every life in the land." [42]

Betrayed by Brown and his men, emissars of the dark powers of evil which he could not identify at the decisive moment because he could not find his own identity in the struggle between heroism and cowardice, Jim realizes that he has come to the wall. He had once "retreated from one world, for a small matter of an impulsive jump, and now the other, the work of his own hands, had fallen in ruins upon his head." [43] In the same moment he decided that he will "defy the disaster," [44] that the "dark powers should not rob him twice of his peace." [45] He knows that everything "was gone, and he who had been once unfaithful to his trust had lost again all men's confidence." [46] And he is all alone. Nobody can understand him. "Loneliness was closing on him." [47] He has no alternative. Nothing can divert him from the only course left. The entreaty of his wife Jewel to stay and fight for his life, his own promise never to desert her, cannot stop him. He has renounced everything earth might have held for him for the sake of preserving his dreams of himself intact. He surrenders himself with the words: "I am come in sorrow. . . . I am come ready and unarmed!" He pays the price at once. "The crowd, which had fallen apart behind Jim as soon as Doramin had raised his hand, rushed tumultuously forward after the shot. They say that the white man sent right and left at all those faces a proud and unflinching glance. Then with his hand over his lips he fell forward, dead." [48]

Jim is young—he is only twenty-four—and he has a rich imagination. It is his imagination that has made him wish to go to sea, it is also his imagination that has prevented him from acting in accordance with his heroic dreams. The vision of the eight hundred people fighting in terror of death for those seven boats made him take the fatal jump, "into a well—into an everlasting deep hole. . . ." [49] Jim is lacking in that "stiffness" a man on the street unaffected with ideas would have shown in a moment of stress. And Conrad means us to see that this is not only Jim's case. To Marlow it is "as if the obscure truth involved were momentous enough to affect mankind's conception of itself. . . ." [50] Something seems wrong with mankind's conception of itself. Just because he is blessed with a more refined sensibility, Jim carries on his back the special burden of humanity. His mind derives its power from the conscious intellect as well as from the irrational subconscious where imagination begins its flights. He would have acted on the simple natural impulse if there had been nothing between the stimulus and his own naked being. But so would Hamlet: "Thus conscience does make cowards of us all." [51]

Man's is a complicated psychology. Consciousness, conscience—we need both words to intervene against direct reflexive action responding to a motive, a stimulus. Conscious life is guided as much by man's rational being abiding on the surface as by the irrational one hidden within, as unfathomable and immense as the universe around him. Jim lives in a world of dreams and tries, by violence, to adapt the world of reality to it. He is unable to look life in the face and see it as it is. Even after the disaster he persists in his dreams. He insists he "had been trapped." [52] "Everything had betrayed him!" [53] It came on him unexpectedly, on a calm night, and took him by surprise. The concerted powers of a malevolent providence have united against the heroic young man to destroy him. But he will never accept their challenge. He will show the world what he really is. He cannot concede his guilt.

Jim has no courage to look into himself. After the

disaster on the sea he may, and he does, develop extreme valor and physical daring, but he never musters enough courage to admit the existence of a dark side to his own personality. Could he but admit it he might have killed the spectre of his past and created a new reality for himself. He need not have abandoned his ideal of chivalrous conduct. But he could not do it. Therefore there is a profound gap in his life, a split in his being, whose very existence depends on internal continuity. The courage he both professes and practices stops at the walls of his external, physical being. Therefore his whole existence stops there, too. This is why nobody can come near him, neither his greatest friends and benefactors, Marlow and Stein, nor his devoted wife, Jewel. He escapes them. When Marlow thinks of Patusan he can remember all the figures, he sees them vividly, but Jim escapes him as though a symbol only and not a physical being.

> The immense and magnanimous Doramin and his little motherly witch of a wife . . . Cornelius, leaning his forehead against the fence under the moonlight—I am certain of them. They exist as if under an enchanter's wand. But the figure round which all these are grouped—that one lives, and I am not certain of him. No magician's wand can immobilise him under my eyes.[54]

To Marlow Jim has been "overwhelmed by the inexplicable . . . by his own personality—the gift of that destiny which he had done his best to master." [55]

Again the tragic necessity of self-knowledge—"gnothi seauton"—is asserted. Jim has ignored this elementary principle imposed on mankind together with the gift of consciousness—and so he is eventually overtaken by his own dark self, whose existence he refused to acknowledge. Symbolically the author often sets him against a dark background, darkness symbolizing the unknown, deeply buried, destructive inner being. Since he cannot reconcile the two elements in his being, he is divided against himself.

Conrad reminds us that this again is universal; "no

man ever understands quite his own artful dodges to escape from the grim shadow of self-knowledge." [56] Jim does his utmost to counteract the inward unease by outward assurance. Talking to Marlow about his position in Patusan, he says: "If you ask them who is brave —who is true—who is just—who is it they would trust with their lives?—they would say, Tuan Jim." [57] Referring to the past in the vaguest terms he almost admits: "I talk about being done with it—with the bally thing at the back of my head . . . Forgetting. . . . Hang me if I know!" And then immediately hushes this remote voice: "I can think of it quietly. After all, what has it proved? Nothing." [58] His whole life is a prolonged attempt to conceal himself from himself: "I must go on, go on forever holding up my end, to feel sure that nothing can touch me." [59] On the surface he has found his peace; his life has become harmonious because his dream, his delusions about himself, seem to have merged with reality. He is the respected "Tuan Jim," the hero, almost more than a mortal. Still, the unadmitted guilt rankless within. He knows that the world he comes from is closed to him and yet he would like that world to know that he is different. He is "like a little child," [60] as though by shutting his eyes he may become invisible to others. He refuses, in effect, to grow out of his youthful daydreams. He does not want to suspect the snake in the bush and so must become its prey.

Jim is human in his rejection of anything less than a complete, integral dream. "A man that is born falls into a dream," [61] as Stein put it, and sinks into it as if into a sea. To this dream that life is, we are to submit ourselves wholly. "Live all you can," as Henry James's Strether advises little Bilham; live as full a life as is offered us, with all our senses exposed to its vibrations. If we don't, if we seek any exemption from the destructive element of life in which we have our being, we are undone. Once Jim had refused to immerse himself, and he paid a high price. The next time he was faced with the same challenge, with the necessity to look into his own darkness and accept himself, was when he was confronted with Captain Brown, the embodiment of the "destructive element" in man himself. Again he refused and missed the chance of getting the spectre of his past by the throat and strangling it. Perhaps this was his opportunity, but it had come veiled and he did not recognize it. Brown gives him a "lesson." His massacre of Jim's people is "a retribution," Marlow says, "a demonstration of some obscure and awful attribute of our nature which, I am afraid, is not so very far under the surface as we like to think." [62]

After Brown had betrayed Jim's trust and so allowed Jim to betray his people, Jim cannot fight for his life because it would lead him the way Brown has gone. It would mean giving in to his dark self, which he stubbornly ignores. The ultimate refusal to accept oneself is tantamount to a rejection of life, an acceptance of death. In Jim's case—as in that of Hamlet—death is a triumph. Hamlet asks Horatio to live in order to tell his story:

> Horatio, I am dead;
> Thou liv'st; report me and my cause aright
> To the unsatisfied.[63]

He does not think he has lived in vain, he is not indifferent to life and the future. Jim's last glance triumphantly runs from face to face as though challenging anyone to call him a coward. He failed in life, but he triumphs in death. Death was his supreme opportunity, it has come to him as "an Eastern bride . . . veiled," [64] but this time he has recognized and followed it.

As though feeling that he has not made it clear enough that, if Jim does represent mankind in its dilemma, his example is not to be followed, Conrad makes him leave "under a cloud." Jewel will not forgive his blindness, his madness in following a dream—she does not know how apt her diagnosis is—and leaving her to whom he has vowed faithfulness. Jim dies to prove that he is true to his pledge, true to his ideal of behavior. Yet those closest to him think him false for this very reason. There again he represents the tragic enigma of life and

poses an eternal question. To whom do we owe allegiance in moments of trial? Is it to an abstract conception of human conduct, or to those most closely associated with us?

Conrad's Jim raises fundamental issues of human behavior. Faust, Hamlet, the parables of the Bible, pictures
of devils and angels fighting for the possession of man's
soul, come to mind. All this has not been casually invented, nor is the tasting of the forbidden fruit in Eden a
story without a lasting relevance. Once man has become
separated from the rest of the "mute creation" he has
taken on the burden of consciousness. He has been
evicted from the paradise where he lived without being
aware of it, like other living beings, and thrown into a
world where he had to control his own life and make his
own choices, directed by the consciousness of himself as
existing. The consequence is a rift in man's being between what used to be called the "spiritual" and the
"physical" elements, or rather the conscious [*ego*] and
the unconscious [*anima, id*]. The unconscious is con-
trolled by the conscious and the conscious is governed by
the influence of the unconscious. They form a whole,
they are inseparable, but they do not easily work together or combine into a harmonious entity. Yet on their
fusion depends the possibility of completeness. And it is
only a complete man, we think, who can establish a
satisfactory relationship with others, with the world he
lives in, and accept the universe he is confronted with.
Only a man in harmony with himself will be relieved
from the curse that follows from self-alienation. Such
internal harmony is the *conditio sine qua non* of that
"happiness" man is always in search of.

Each of us is prompted by constructive, life-giving
urges, just as none is free from destructive, negative ones.
There is good and bad in each of us. This a commonplace—as it is also a commonplace to say that we must
bring our divided selves into a condition of harmony.
But Conrad goes deeper into the matter and sees that
man's rational and irrational potentialities, inextricably

combined in his being, make him a personality that diverges considerably from the prevailing ideas about man. He has discovered this through watching closely the people around him as they were confronted with the cosmic element of the sea: "Trust a boat on the high seas to bring out the Irrational that lurks at the bottom of every thought, sentiment, sensation, emotion." [65] He has realized the omnipresence of the irrational, which pervades every human being, enters all his pores, all his atoms, his rational, emotional, and sensual being. Conrad had the courage to admit and accept what he saw. The shipwreck of the *Patna* is not the only shipwreck: "there are as many shipwrecks as there are men." [66]

2

Ursula Brangwen

> "It isn't the being that must follow the mind, but the mind must follow the being." [1]

D. H. Lawrence's idea that the function of art is "to reveal the relation between man and his circumambient universe, at the living moment"; [2] his conception of the novel "as the one bright book of life" which, unlike "poetry, philosophy, science or any other book-tremulation . . . can make the whole man alive tremble"; [3] his attitude to human personality as expressed in the characters of his novels and his suggestion that the reader should not look for the "old stable ego" of conventional fiction set him apart from most of the novelists and artists of his time. His concentration on the much larger area of being below the surface, his evocation of the subconscious, together with his determination to make this his field of exploration, opened a new vision of man and enabled him as a novelist to penetrate into the human mind further than practically any of his contemporaries. He stood so far in the forefront of his time as almost to lose touch with the main guard. Separated from the bulk of the army, D. H. Lawrence had to battle at times all alone on a hitherto untrodden path leading through a jungle of unsorted growths to a clearing and to those unconstricted horizons that would open to release him for his major work.

The early novels, especially *Sons and Lovers* [1913] were a kind of testing ground. Writing that novel, he was fighting for his freedom, fighting for a soul still jealously guarded by his mother. While tearing himself out of

that close embrace, to which all his emotional being had
been geared, Lawrence emancipated himself from the
ethical assumptions of his time and place. Once he could
immolate the dominant mother figure, he could destroy
all the other gods. Then he was free to undertake the
pilgrimage of his life, disregarding everything but his
own permanently changing, expanding vision of life,
moving towards an ever richer, because profounder, conception of human personality.

It is woman that has, in D. H. Lawrence's view, retained the closer link with nature. It is therefore natural
that he should have given the fullest statement of what
he sees as the essential conflict through which a harmony
can be established with oneself and correspondingly
with nature and the living universe, in the figure of a
woman rather than a man. Ursula of *The Rainbow*
[1915] and its sequel *Women in Love* [1920] holds a
central place in Lawrence's work. She exemplified her
author's idea of human personality at the time he was
making a first full effort to formulate a conception of
the function of man in life. By following the general
pattern of life in the animate world, by complementing
his own being in relationship with the other sex, one
could reach fulfillment, unite, and yet remain separate.
For it was, as D. H. Lawrence thought, by subsiding into
the rhythm of the unconscious living world that one's
conscious being, one's mind, is released, and one gains
full freedom.

Although Ursula's story seems to end on a note of
defeat, it is in her figure that Lawrence has most completely embodied his conception of man. Ursula was
created before his developing passion to escape contemporary society had led him to create an artificial world in
which his rebel exiles could deploy without interference
their pent-up external and social being.

There are few characters in the English novel or indeed
anywhere whom we meet the very first day they are born

and of whose antecedents we are as precisely informed as we are with Ursula. We learn about her ancestry, the two preceding generations of the Brangwens, and about the growth of the family and the transformation of the soil they cultivated and into which they sent their roots just as deeply as the trees they had themselves planted. From her emergence into a world baffling in its confusion of passion and antagonistic conflict, Ursula appears as part of the living cosmos, a component in the dark profundities of nature to which she will inevitably owe allegiance just as much as to the world created by men.

Ursula is born to Anna and Will Brangwen when they are still very young—Anna nineteen, Will just over twenty. Their violent struggle for supremacy has not yet come to any resolution. For Anna this struggle is channelled in motherhood; for Will, in a withdrawal from "daylight" into a dark inner world of sensuality and passion:

> she was the daytime, the daylight, he was the shadow, put aside, but in the darkness potent with an overwhelming voluptuousness . . .
> So they remained as separate in the light, and in the thick darkness, married. He supported her daytime authority, kept it inviolable at last. And she, in all the darkness, belonged to him, to his close, insinuating, hypnotic familiarity.[4]

Anna is the central link in Will's life; his daily existence is filled with lonely hard work to keep the growing family going. But both partners' progress towards full articulateness through a creative fulfilment—to use the author's language—in mutual love and understanding, has been barred by this division, and barred for life. They remain "uncreated." Anna's more satisfactory refuge, her motherhood, allows her to postpone her growth and "begin to grow up again only with her youngest child."[5] This possibility is not open to Will, and so he refuses to be brought to full consciousness. In the advent of the first child, Ursula, he finds an outlet for the pent-up intensity of his emotional being. He waits impatiently for the time the child will be passed on from her mother's care to himself, when the mother expecting the next child will turn her attention away from the first-born.

> So . . . the father had the elder baby, the weaned child, golden-brown, wondering vivid eyes of the little Ursula were for him, who had waited behind the mother till the need was for him. The mother felt a sharp stab of jealousy . . .
> So Ursula became the child of her father's heart. She was the little blossom, he was the sun. He was patient, energetic, inventive for her. He taught her all the funny little things, he filled her and roused her to her fullest tiny measure. She answered him with her extravagant infant's laughter and her call of delight.[6]

Ursula grows into a hypersensitive child. Through her young father's influence she soon becomes aware of the world in which she moves. A lace designer in Nottingham, Will Brangwen's greatest passion is wood carving, his deepest interest church architecture and painting and their history. But he must work in the garden encircling the cottage at Cossethay, plant, dig, grow vegetables, provide for the growing family in more ways than one. His greatest attachment, the very habitat of his dark being, becomes the church close to the house. He keeps it in repair, attends to the organ he plays, sees to the woodwork. The toddling child follows her father like a shadow. So she is initiated into his solitary double existence divided between communion with nature, whose changing seasons she begins to notice before she becomes aware of herself, and a passionate love of the church. The dark Gothic church seems to envelop the mystery of life, to cultivate the eternal wonder at the miracle of human existence, as reflected in the recurrent rituals of the Christian year. In this intense atmosphere Ursula is too soon awakened, emerging "almost in pain from the transient unconsciousness of childhood. Wide-eyed, unseeing, she was awake before she knew how to see." [7] Living in her own world, where alone she "was always herself," she feels the world outside to be accidental.[8] She can retain and nurture her own individual propensities, and continue as a being deeply rooted in the soil; she lives with nature and shares in the ecstasy of the flower opening in spring under the caress of the sun. Unhindered by the pressure of conventional life she can flourish into a full human being.

Her father is the only person to occupy "any permanent position in the childish consciousness,"[9] and his influence does not take the child out of its world. As "a piece of light that really belonged to him, that played within his darkness,"[10] she can let her own darkness have free play. Her mind can "follow her being" long enough to establish a firm link between her daylight being, existing on the surface, and the dark subterranean one, the unconscious, submerged like an iceberg only a small part of which floats above the surface of the ocean. Firmly rooted in her own being, she will avoid the pitfalls of incomplete relationship and finally build an adequate union with the man who promises to be a deserving partner. The story of Ursula's life centres on her attempt to find through union with such a man the "creative fulfillment" that would open her way to a full life, make her free to create her life, give it the "moral form" that suits her being. For according to Lawrence, "every man . . . must be an artist in life, must create his own moral form." Everybody should master the "art of living," which is "harder than the art of writing."[11]

If "the germ of this novel," as the author says, is "woman becoming individual, self-responsible, taking her own initiative,"[12] it is not the whole of the novel. The prominence given to Ursula's earliest awareness of herself, her formation, makes it more than that. *The Rainbow* is one of the freshest and most original explorations into the growth of a child's mind in modern literature, and it was written at a time when the paramount importance of the child's earliest experiences was not yet well understood. It is likewise the first novel that follows the lines of modern psycho-analytical thinking. The salient features of Ursula's personality stand out early in her childhood. If they become more prominent as she grows, they do not fundamentally change. She is imaginative, susceptible to the influence of atmosphere both in nature and among people, and yet there is a firm core in her which remains separate, which does not allow anything from the alien world to do violence to her inmost being. The greatest influence at this stage comes from her father. She adores him, but he, "walking in his own darkness, not in anybody else's world at all," [13] forgets that she is only a little child and hurts her and makes her close herself against him. Still she clings to him. His separateness, his profoundly religious attitude to life, his aloofness from the world at large are attractive to Ursula, who early shrank from the simple people she had to mix with at Cossethay. "She had an instinctive fear of petty people, as a deer is afraid of dogs." [14] Her father, Lawrence tells us, could still fit her illusion of a man "whose life was an Odyssey in an outer world." [15]

Ursula's grandmother with her Polish background, her refinement, her mysterious youth spent in a remote and picturesque country, also appealed to the child. Her contact with the old woman leaves its mark. It meant not only an escape from her Cossethay home where "all was activity and passion, everything moved upon poles of passion . . . a throng of babies, all the time many lives beating against each other." [16] She enjoyed the peace of her grandmother's bedroom: here she "came as to a hushed, paradisal land, here her own existence became simple and exquisite to her as if she were a flower." [17] Talking as though to herself the old woman often lost sight of Ursula. The little girl learnt that there were things that went beyond our immediate mortal life and that it depended on oneself whether one would get them or not. She heard that her grandfather Tom Brangwen got them, because he "had served her."

> He had come to her, and taken from her. He had died and gone his way into death. But he had made himself immortal in his knowledge with her. So she had her place here,

in life, and in immortality. For he had taken his knowledge of her into death, so that she had her place in
death.[18]

Ursula heard, too, how her actual grandfather, her
mother's Polish father, had failed because he had
thought that he was "the beginning and the end." He
had taken too much upon himself and died a bitter man.

At the time when an impressionable, imaginative
child avidly takes cognizance of things, Ursula could talk
to her grandmother, ask her all those questions children
must have answered:

> "Will somebody love me, grandmother?"
> "Many people love you, child. We all love you."
> "But when I am grown up, will somebody love me?"
> "Yes, some man will love you, child, because it's your
> nature. And I hope it will be somebody who will love you
> for what you are, and not for what he wants of you. But
> we have a right to what we want." [19]

However much a world of illusion like Ursula's might
be at variance with reality, it could have a stimulative
effect in her adolescence. It would prepare her to spread
her wings for the greatest flight in her life. On these
aspiring imaginary flights often depends the magnitude
of the ventures of one's mature life. For if not wide off
the young being's possibilities, they mark the limits of
the highest goal one may attain in adult life. The substance of one's youthful aspirations changes, the intensity carries over. On it depends the adolescent's efforts to
realize his early dream. Only if one's strivings go wholly
beyond one's reach, and so can never fuse with one's
reality, are they harmful. In Ursula's case, they stimulated her to persist in her endeavours to find a form of
life that would suit her, in which her dreams would
materialize and her world of imagination merge with
reality.

It is therefore natural that she should resent her
school's matter of factness, and repudiate a religion
which would deprive her of her personal, sensual experi-

ence of Christianity. While still lonely and holding her own end against a hostile, malevolent world, with nothing but antagonism for her mother and with a passionate love and mistrust of her father, she tried to find in the "cycle of creation" [20] the hidden meaning of life. She lived through the weekdays almost automatically: attended school, acquired knowledge, but all the time combatted the teaching, the influence of school, that would break through her world of fantasy in which miracles could still happen. While living for the Sundays and the performance of the Church's rituals and myths, which allowed her to identify herself with the "daughters of men" waiting for the "Sons of God," Ursula imperceptibly drifted into young womanhood. When she took up teaching she ran up against a rational, formalized, rigid system in which the individual child was ignored, antagonized and then made to learn by force dead matter deprived of all living value. Her whole being rebelled against it, but she would not give in. One of the new generation of emancipated women—she belongs to her own generation, which lends her meaning on yet another level—she assumes the repulsive role she is given. She would not allow the children to get the better of her, or her fellow-teachers and the headmaster to see her fail.

When she enters the University of Nottingham at the age of nineteen, she is still the dreamy aspiring young being who cannot allow life to be reduced to the drabness of reality but must invest it in glamor, lend it the spiritual quality of some kind of miracle. Together with her sister Gudrun she explores this new world:

> The two girls were distinguished wherever they went, slim, strong girls, eager and extremely sensitive . . .
>
> Ursula was much more carefully dressed, but she was selfconscious, always falling into depths of admiration of somebody else, and modelling herself upon this other, and so producing a hopeless incongruity. When she dressed for practical purposes she always looked well. In winter, wearing a tweed coat-and-skirt, and a small hat of black

fur pulled over her eager, palpitant face, she seemed to move down the street in a drifting motion of suspense and exceeding sensitive receptivity.[21]

As though to protect her own internal separateness Ursula tries not to diverge from others in her clothes. And yet in everything else how persistently she goes after the meaning that things, according to her, should have. For her the university, in spite of its ugly Gothic arches, held "a reminiscence of the wondrous, cloistral origin of education."[22] She felt as though she were "within the great, whispering sea-shell, that whispered all the while with reminiscence of all the centuries, [where] time faded away, and the echo of knowledge filled the timeless silence."[23] Lecturers appeared to her as "black-gowned priests of knowledge, serving for ever in a remote and hushed temple. They were the initiated, and the beginning and the end of the mystery was in their keeping."[24] But the rational narrow assurance of the teachers, whose world of vision stopped on the confines of the visible and palpable, soon alienated her. Being herself aware of darkness, with all its terror of the unknown and the unknowable

> she felt the strange, foolish vanity of the camp, which said "Beyond our light and our order there is nothing," turning their faces always inward towards the sinking fire of illuminating consciousness, which comprised sun and stars and the Creator, and the System of Righteousness, ignoring always the vast darkness that wheeled round about, with half-revealed shapes lurking on the edge.[25]

Now everything the university can offer seems meretricious. She is disappointed in her expectations. The same pattern seems to run throughout her childhood and youth: the alien, cruel world, depersonalized and artificial, forcing itself on the world of imagination and gaining ground against it. And yet she knows and feels all the time that the "arc lamp" of consciousness mankind is so proud of represents but a small part of everything there is in this world, which man can explore and discover more through insight and faith than through intellect and machinery.

The central preoccupation of Ursula's life, to find out for herself what life can offer her and how she can respond to it—or, better, how she should attune herself to her own being so as to respond to it most directly without interference of anything alien, imposed by a civilization that antagonizes her—first led to an early involvement with a young man. Anton Skrenbensky's Polish descent appealed to the girl of sixteen who had discovered the land of his origin in the stories of her grandmother. Anton could fit into the world of her fantasy, and yet even at that tender age, and in spite of her youthful infatuation, she senses that something she is in search of is not there. It is only later, when she meets him at the age of twenty-two, that she is struck by something in his appearance that puts her off: "It was no use turning with flesh and blood to this arrangement of forged metal." [26] Her insight, fostered by frequent sojourns in her inner darkness, tells her that he is cold, all dead inside. Her yearning youth, her potent sensual being will have satisfaction. She throws herself into a sensual feast with Anton. They live for their love. Anton for once forgets his daylight being, his social, conventional no-being, and lives for his own darkness, sharing it richly with Ursula.

Free from themselves, from all convention, united in a powerful physical embrace in a world that belongs to them, both lovers experience complete ecstasy. Having entirely surrendered to the more powerful personality of Ursula, Anton suggests after a few months that they should get married. This brings their hitherto dark relationship up into the world of convention in which Anton is a different, strange person, alien to Ursula. She is attached to him, she pities him for his dependence on her, but she must follow her insight, her "being" and refuse him. She cannot attach her life to a man who is unable to be himself, who is not complete and so cannot offer himself as an equal partner to a woman. Anton cannot come to creative fulfillment through love with a woman just as he cannot establish a harmonious contact with his own deeper self, with his unconscious, through which alone he can become complete.

Alone in a world where women are just beginning to assert their equality, in a home where virginity is held high, Ursula awakes with horror to the possibility that she might be with child by Anton. This, together with the perspective of a vast unknown stretching infinitely ahead of her, with the security of conventional life she might have had with Anton rejected, causes a nervous breakdown. For a while her mind seems almost obscured by erotic nightmares. Figuratively speaking she dies, but she is not defeated, so she must rise from her ashes. She emerges a maturer personality. Her hope for the future, for the transformation of the ugly mining settlement—the mine as a symbol for the impoverishment of human life in an industrialized community runs like a permanent motif through both novels—and for the growth of men into independent and powerful individuals, is matched with her own growth. She begins to realize what she expects of life. In spite of the terror she feels at times, the recurring "horror of the husk which bound in her and all mankind" and her sense that they "were all in prison, they were all going mad," [27] she is convinced that there is something in man that will conquer the barriers he himself has erected against his own full and natural existence. The rainbow in the sky—the leading symbol in the novel—seems to span not only the opposing poles of a corrupted and a fulfilled life, of man and woman meeting in the midst of the unbroken arch; it also indicates the possibility of achieving harmony, and holds hope of a better future for mankind.

Ursula's formation has reached an end. And *The Rainbow* duly ends here. But Ursula's story must continue until she has achieved the consummation of her being as a woman. Her determination to accept nothing but an absolute fulfillment in her personal life has brought her a heroic victory accompanied by its concomitant—loneliness. The author must explore and see what life has in store for her early in this century.

At the age of twenty-six Ursula and her sister Gudrun share "the remote virgin look of modern girls, sisters of Artemis rather than of Hebe." [28] Ursula, with her look of "sensitive expectancy" expressive of her profound inner mood, has about her, always,

> that strange brightness of an essential flame that was caught, meshed, contravened. She lived a good deal by herself, to herself, working, passing on from day to day, and always thinking, trying to lay hold on life, to grasp it in her own understanding. Her active living was suspended, but underneath, in the darkness, something was coming to pass. If only she could break through the last integuments! She seemed to try and put her hands out, like an infant in the womb, and she could not, not yet. Still she had a strange prescience, an intimation yet to come.[29]

Ursula's life has assumed a monotonous rhythm. She teaches botany and brings at least the immediacy of nature to her pupils. But her personal being is repressed; it is there invisible below the surface, on its guard, lying in wait for one of the "Sons of God."

The encounter with Rupert Birkin opens Ursula's way to a further exploration of her own yearnings. Birkin knows what he wants, or he thinks he does. His exclamation, "I only want us to *know* what we are," [30] shows a determination to find out both what he is and what he wants. His bitter experience with Hermione, a woman governed by intellect and will, has shown him the desert life can become when the instinctual dark being, suppressed, comes forth again in a maniacal obsession to possess and subdue to one's will the person one loves. Birkin yearns for a woman he can love freely, without having to possess or be possessed. His goal, his only salvation in life, becomes union with such a woman. In Ursula he sees the woman with whom he may experience the kind of love through which both partners will gain their freedom, retain their separateness and yet become one and establish a world together. His activity as school inspector, in a world guided by will and subjected to mechanisms created by the intellect, becomes increasingly odious to him.

Ursula, however, is not ready to comply with Birkin's rigid conception of impersonal love. She calls him a prophet—and here Lawrence is laughing at himself. They clash. Like her mother before her, she cannot imagine love without taking possession of the man, asserting her own supremacy over his as woman. After more than one conflict, and protracted periods of antagonism, they find a way to each other. Each discovers in the other what he had expected of this, the most profound contact given to man.

> She looked at him. He seemed still so separate. New eyes were opened in her soul. She saw a strange creature from another world, in him. It was as if she were enchanted, and everything were metamorphosed. She recalled again the old magic of the Book of Genesis, where the sons of God saw the daughters of men, that they were fair. And he was one of these, one of these strange creatures from the beyond, looking down at her, and seeing she was fair.
>
> He stood on the hearth-rug looking at her, at her face that was upturned exactly like a flower, a fresh, luminous flower, glinting faintly golden with the dew of the first light. And he was smiling faintly as if there were no speech in the world, save the silent delight of flowers in each other. Smilingly they delighted in each other's presence, pure presence, not to be thought of, even known.[31]

Both their conscious and unconscious beings are equally engaged in their ultimate discovery of and union with each other. Through this mutual consummation they are at one with nature, in unison with the living world, in harmony with themselves and the universe.

Union with man has been the culminating point of Ursula's being, the chief motif of the story, the goal toward which her growth into womanhood had led. What follows is no longer Ursula's story, it does not contribute to her character. Ursula is there, as complete as the author could make her, for the common reader to accept or reject as a reflection of the modern woman "becoming individual, self-responsible, taking her own initiative." [32]

It is Ursula more than any character in the modern English novel before her that reveals the *being*, the unconscious, buried beneath the consciousness that is displayed in our surface life. The chief stages of her growth are offered to the reader in a story that might have formed a *künstlerroman*, a novel presenting the growth of an artist's character, if, in accordance with the author's dictum, we accept Ursula's untiring endeavor to find a "moral form" for her life as an artistic activity and the life she finally creates with Birkin as an artifact. But it is always Ursula's *being* that is kept in the reader's eye, and the inner struggle of that being to retain supremacy over her consciousness. The envelope in which her being is wrapped is likewise kept clearly in view, but the further we follow her progress the less aware we are of Ursula as a full character. The dark unknown to which the author has given prominence seems to penetrate from underneath and, like a mist, cover the outlines of her individuality. Yet should not this individuality have been the author's chief concern? For how can she be herself, separate and unique—and everything in the novel, as indeed in life, depends on this—once she becomes all women and loses in that degree her distinct personality?

Ursula is, however, something more than a projection of the eternal feminine. She is not only woman incarnate, she also conveys the author's idea of life and human existence. She voices his defiance of the existing modern world whose tendency towards self-destruction Lawrence felt as so directly immanent that it could not but be incorporated in his characters. His awareness of the unconscious, the "unknown modes of being," and his exploration of the hitherto hardly mentioned depths of personal being submerged beneath the smooth surface of life, together with his rejection of the "stable ego," in which, as he told Edward Garnett, he had lost interest,[33] bring him close to the world of Dostoevsky's imagination —a world Lawrence himself had vehemently repudiated at the time of *The Rainbow*, but fervently acclaimed on the eve of his death.[34] D. H. Lawrence's characters, his whole world, are enveloped in a special atmosphere; a "medium"—to borrow a term applied by Isiah Berlin to the case of *War and Peace*. This "medium" in which Isaiah Berlin says, we are "immersed and submerged," and which we therefore "cannot observe as if from the outside; cannot identify, measure and seek to manipulate," [35] is exactly where Lawrence's characters have their common being, where they exist on the unconscious level, while retaining their conscious outward personality.[36] Here they appear free agents of themselves. This is the area that Lawrence explored. First in the field, he shares in the triumphs and limitations of the pioneer, who, while breaking a new path in one direction, almost inevitably loses sight of the whole. Like H. G. Wells, Lawrence in his own way—is it the case with self-made men?—began to allow the voice of the prophet to dominate his novels. It was not enough for him to explore, reveal, and communicate; he must teach and rescue blundering mankind from a course leading to destruction.

According to Lawrence, Ursula is the foremost case in his fiction, the individual's whole free being leads one more surely than the mind. Ursula does not subject herself to her intellect, or to her will. Without posing as a rebel she complies with the order of the world the least she can. As a girl of seventeen, even before she independently steps out into the modern world of man's making, she realizes the destructiveness of the industrial and social organization symbolized by the mine.

> The pit was the great mistress. Ursula looked out of the window and saw the proud, demonlike colliery with her wheels twinkling in the heavens, the formless, squalid mass of the town lying aside. It was the squalid heap of

> side-shows. The pit was the main show, the *raison d'être of all*.
>
> How terrible it was! There *was* a horrible fascination in it,—human bodies and lives subjected in slavery to that symmetric monster of the colliery . . . No more would she subscribe to the great colliery, to the great machine which has taken us all captives. In her soul, she was against it, she disowned even its power.[37]

She revolts against the idea that life should be a "side-show," that human life should be subjected to an abstract machine, not less because it is a machine invented by the human mind and imposed by the human will.

The fact that Ursula is an optimistic idealist, that she never loses hope for the future, is again, according to the author, typically feminine, the woman as child-bearer being closer to the fountain of life and therefore more open to life's reviving influence. Ursula hopes that man will finally reject the mechanical life he has created and build a world that will be fully human and in harmony with his deepest aspiration. On this optimistic note ends Ursula's young womanhood, on the last page of *The Rainbow*.

> And the rainbow stood on the earth. She knew that the sordid people who crept hard-scaled and separate on the face of the world's corruption were living still, that the rainbow was arched in their blood and would quiver to life in their spirit, that they would cast off their horny covering of disintegration, that new, clean, naked bodies would issue to a new germination, to a new growth, rising to the light and the wind and the clean rain of heaven. She saw in the rainbow the earth's new architecture, the old, brittle corruption of houses and factories swept away, the world built up in a living fabric of Truth, fitting to the over-arching heaven.[38]

This vision, we note, embodies no particular revolutionary scheme. For the same reason that she rebels against the machine of modern life, Ursula suspects mass movements, even the feminist one in which she, as one of her generation, in actual fact participates. Everything that is collective and overlooks the individual rouses her doubts. She feels that each of us is and should be different, unique as an individual. She has no confidence in mass solutions, collective arrangements. She knows that each of us should build his own life freely, strive to find a form to express himself more fully. Therefore she is also suspicious of democracy:

> "I shall be glad to leave England. Everything is so meagre and paltry, it is so unspiritual—I hate democracy!"
> "What do you mean?" he [Anton] asked her, hostile. "Why do you hate democracy?"
> "Only the greedy and ugly people come to the top in democracy," she said, "because they're the only people who will push themselves there. Only degenerate races are democratic."
> "What do you want then—an aristocracy?"
> "I *do* want an aristocracy," she cried. "And I'd far rather have an aristocracy of birth than of money. Who are the aristocrats now—who are chosen as the best to rule? Those who have money and the brains for money. It doesn't matter what else they have: but they must have money-brains,—because they are ruling in the name of money." [39]

Ursula dreads a world subjected to money and ruled by a technocracy, in which the individual is treated as a number in the statistics, his individual claims so far neglected that he himself forgets he should have any, the needs of his existence reduced to vulgar collective welfare.

Ursula is finally able to achieve the ultimate blending of the female with the male being that opens the door to the world beyond, the world of miracle, because she has kept the innermost flame of her being alive. Through her communion with nature, she has always felt she belonged to this further world, and through a full-hearted participation in the annual cycle of the Christian year, she had retained the childlike wonder at the magic, the eternal mystery of life. According to Lawrence, a harmonious human development requires not only closeness to nature, a participation in the dense atmosphere or "medium" of the collective unconscious. It likewise requires the cultivation of conscious faith in something beyond practical vulgar reality, be it through Christian or some other myths. Such a rich, unhindered growth, where imagination, senses, and intellect are equally nourished, can lead to a harmonious union of woman with man, through which human participation in nature is reasserted, the "miracle of life" accepted and the flame of spiritual energy, going beyond the span of individual life, firmly sustained. This course, that keeps man above the level of brute animal existence, is doggedly followed by Ursula, however lonely it had been at times. Her faith in the value of human life and the living world has never wavered.

Yet in the end the young couple choose exile. In a sense they reject the world. Birkin wants to create an artificial circle where they might exercise their outward social being. He seems to ignore the truth that one's internal state does depend on the state of life outside. We cannot hope to exist harmoniously within ourselves unless we equally exist in the society we commonly inhabit. An artist of D. H. Lawrence's power could not but feel this, although he was obviously not ready to face the full consequences at that stage of his life [we may remember, too, that he wrote out Ursula's story during the early years of the First World War]. Ursula as a character in fiction, and indeed as an imaginable person in reality, is no exception to this rule. It is an impalpable rule, and yet it governs our lives as firmly as Archimedes' rule of displacement. If the balance of the outer tension between self and society is tipped, there is no internal equilibrium that will not also suffer. This is where the existentialist theory of the inevitability of commitment proves true. One is committed, one's actions are "engaged," by the very fact that one is alive and exists. One can only exist on both planes, the inward and personal and the outward and social.

Ursula's final triumph in personal life, her victory on one plane, is ironically matched by failure on another. It is as though the author's advance through the hitherto barely suspected regions of the unconscious had deluded him into believing that this was all that finally mattered and that, united on this plane, man and woman would have solved the riddle of human life. He seems to have forgotten that the challenge of life in the outward world of human action requires just as much of each of us as the challenge of our internal being. Ursula, who in accordance with Lawrence's own theories, being grown into womanhood, should have opened the man's way, too, into the common world of men and women, the world at large, is deprived of that role. For all his efforts to make her a living character beyond any novelist before him, Lawrence has finally failed to make her complete in action. Viewed as a character in the novel Ursula does not fully live up to the goal the author set himself.

3

Stephen Dedalus

> Welcome, O life! I go to encounter for the millionth time the
> reality of experience and to forge in the smithy of my soul the
> uncreated conscience of my race.[1]

The idea of the transformation of, at once, human personality and the general order of life seems to have
found its proper literary instrument in the modern psychological novel, in which the human figure may be
more or less naturalistically broken into pieces and reas-
sembled into a new whole. Through the figure of Stephen Dedalus, James Joyce thus set out to recreate the
world. Stephen is to forge in his own mind—for this is
what "soul," in the metaphor chosen, appears to stand
for—the conscience of his race. Since the word "conscience" is preceded by the adjective "uncreated," the
novelist implies that his is a radically new departure, that
the current ideas about man and his life as a moral being
have been rejected. The artist has taken upon himself
the tremendous task of giving a new beginning to things.
The old conceptions of human personality and of a
universal and objective moral truth being overthrown,
the artist himself has become the only source of truthful
understanding, the only sacred fount on which to draw.
If he is to create a new human figure he can model it
only on himself. Thus he will be deeply involved in his
creation, in the character he builds, however artful he
may be in objectifying it.

The emphasis, through Stephen's words, on the artist
as "the God of creation" is not simply blasphemous
romanticism. It points to Joyce's awareness of the intri-

cacy and magnitude of his task. It reveals his desire to counteract the inevitable subjectivity of his work. He is to withdraw, to separate his creation from himself, whatever it may cost him. But is this undertaking really possible? Can the author so detach himself from his own creation? Can he make the world he creates, the figures he builds, completely independent of his own particular sentient being? The more the artist protests that he is objective, the less he is to be trusted. And it may just be his intuition that the ultimate goal, artistic objectivity, cannot be reached that makes him so insistent upon his own godlike indifference.

The idea of *stasis*, the instant immobilization of things, leading through *epiphany* to the act of creation, draws Joyce away from the novel proper that can thrive and flourish only on living, continuously changing characters. James Joyce, and to a certain extent Virginia Woolf, pose a special problem for this study. The characters they created now appear to us as typical of the period after 1914 whose fatalistic acceptance of the catastrophe of 1914–18 and of the lopsided world that emerged from it led headlong into World War II. Their own separatist attitude to life and human personality prevented them from breathing the atmosphere of common life into their own creations and making them complete. This might seem to disqualify their characters from serving the purposes of an essay of the present kind, but the fact is that their authors' inability to set them free from the act of manipulation that created them was just as typical of the special trials of twentieth-century literature as the incompleteness of the characters elsewhere produced. The characters of Joyce and Virginia Woolf provide a vital if tenuous link in the chain of inquiry into human personality in modern English literature. By sacrificing their own lives, building their own personalities into the offspring of their imagination, these novelists have prevented the human figure from dissolving completely, the chain of continuity from breaking beyond repair.

If James Joyce has created one living character that can serve the purposes of a study of this kind, it is Stephen Dedalus of A *Portrait of the Artist as a Young Man*, more especially if we resort also, as I think is legitimate, to the manuscript that preceded it, *Stephen Hero*. The Stephen of *Ulysses*, together with the other monumental characters of that immense novel, is a comic figure and so inevitably static, apart from being deliberately immobilized, broken up for the inspection the author elaborately holds out to the reader of what goes on inside him. The *Portrait* itself, a veritable *künstlerroman*, does not entirely avoid the pitfalls of its genre. At times too closely associated with the author's own life, it tends elsewhere to counterbalance this by an exaggerated objectivity in concentrating on the special subject of the formation of an artist's mind. We find a fuller naturalistic presentation of Stephen in *Stephen Hero*.[2] The *Portrait* is developed from inside the character's mind, proceeding from his earliest impressions between the ages of two and four or five until he is nineteen. His character consequently is to be felt and apprehended, and thus created as an entity, in the reader's mind. His outward life is not easy to picture in consecutive fashion. It intermittently solidifies and dissolves, like "a train going in and out of tunnels,"[3] each new phase or climax in this associational process of episode and response opening a new avenue into Stephen's mind.

Stephen is a delicate, sensitive, highly strung boy with an imagination that tends to look to legends for an explanation of whatever puzzles him. Very early he finds in words both the stimulation to enter and the landmarks to guide him in the yet undiscovered landscape of the world that stretches further and further ahead as he grows up. Stephen soon begins to diverge from the ways of the world in which he lives. From a quiet, perceptive, intellectually gifted child with a strong sense of justice and the courage to stand up for it, he develops into a young man sure of his vocation as an artist and determined to exercise a complete moral and intellectual freedom. He will repudiate whatever his mind has departed from: "I will not serve that in which I no longer believe." [4] He will freely see and experience life and find the most appropriate artistic device to render, to recreate it; he will, in the words Cranly repeats back to him, "discover the mode of life or of art whereby your spirit could express itself in unfettered freedom." [5] Stephen's story is that of an emancipation from the bonds that would tie him, for the purpose of exploring the world and finding, in terms of his own experience thereof, his own truth about it.

In this sense again Stephen's case is typical of the formation of the young artist's mind, beginning with an almost complete reliance on the given world and ending when he has grown his own wings and can launch out upon the independent flight of his own life. But his is an extreme and violent case. He does not, while in the process of growth, loosen in gradual succession the bonds of family, country, religion, and ethos that the early sections of the novel so vividly present. What we are shown is rather a clamorous repudiation and a loud declaration of immediate and complete independence from whatever he had held in esteem. It is an assertion of his own superiority to his antecedents and an arrogant resolution to dictate his own terms to those he until recently had treated as his superiors, simply in order to do the work he has undertaken. This is as arrogant a declaration of adult freedom as may be imagined. Stephen's is not only a growth toward maturity; [6] it is a shattering revolt against every influence that has moulded him, and a destruction in conscience of the milieu in which he has grown up.

Human birth is a separation and an emancipation from the womb; growth is the drifting away, usually gradual, from the attitudes, ideas, and tenets held and imposed by one's elders, and an attempt to build with one's own generation a slightly or more completely different new world. Not often, however, is the breaking away from the earlier generation as radical and as fully voiced as that of Stephen. Such a furious rejection of the beliefs and ideas in which he had been brought up, to which he, as it seemed, meekly adhered until his adolescence, could have been caused only by special conditions.

The perpetual degradation of his once prosperous and respected family; its falling into ever greater misery; the ejection from one flat after another, always poorer and more squalid; the recklessness of the father, who maintained the prerogative of strict paternal authority without attending to his proper functions as husband, parent, provider, and guardian of his family—all this caused the boy intense suffering. The submissiveness of his mother, who found solace and an escape from humiliations in the paradise promised her by her Church, increasingly irritated the proud young boy as he was growing into manhood. Stephen's egoism, his show of callous indifference and cynicism, grew out of his attempt to protect himself from too painful a spectacle. While still at an age when he could indiscriminately nurse hopes of a sudden miraculous rehabilitation for his decaying family, he had spent the money his essays had won him most generously on his parents and family, but soon this very generosity seemed foolish and contemptible.

Stephen's attitude to his country is inextricable from that to his family. The futile disputes over Parnell he had witnessed as a child, the loud protests of his ineffectual father, the exhortations and lamentations of his parents, friends, and relatives, must have once and for all created in the boy's mind—as in Conrad's before him [7] —an impression of futility concerning his country's future. How could people of so little firmness and determination bring a great future about? In his own house and family he saw patriotism dissolve into powerless rage and hysterical quarrels that seemed to consume all the fire that was in them. Already at sixteen Stephen began to apply his mind and develop his own theories on life and art. These he built into a whole system of self-defense against the humiliations of a blighted and malevolent world, but with these he also ran head-on into the intense resistance of Irish parochialism and narrowmindedness. He was determined not to allow anyone to thwart his drive toward independence. Everybody seemed to be in league against him as a heretic and free thinker. As a result he was repelled by the nascent movement of Irish cultural nationalism. He could not support or take part in a movement in which he could not fully believe. His refusal to join this movement enthusiastically accepted by his fellows intensified the hostility and ill will they felt for this cosmopolitan young man claiming absolute freedom of opinion for himself.

The last and, for a boy of Stephen's education and spirit, most fatal repudiation had to follow. After a serious attempt to comply with the teaching and practice of the Catholic faith and a painful heart-searching confession accompanied by sincere repentance, Stephen suddenly began to feel free from his own religious fervor. The indomitable, uncontrollable impulse of youth, especially powerful in a potential artist, suddenly released him from his mute submission to the Church. The gloomy vision of an eternity of hell and purgatory to which the Church would subject him lost power over his imagination. The offer of the Jesuit fathers to join their order, at first flattering to the pious young man, in the end only intensified his instinct to go his own way. His entire sensuous, emotional, and intellectual being was roused, drawing up from the depths of his hitherto suppressed *self* the first poetic assertion of himself as an artist: "A day of dappled seaborne clouds." [8] Stephen's youthful hymn to life merges here with that of youth in general. "To live, to err, to fall, to triumph, to recreate life out of life!" [9]

Stephen now tries to discover the nature of art and of himself as artist. His mind is steeped in the teaching and trained in the methods of discussion and the catechising exercises of the Catholic Church. His vindication of art and its function therefore derives, as he proudly declares, from St. Aquinas. As artist, as poet, Stephen conceives of himself in the analogy of the God of Creation. He remains, we see, imbued with the "medium" [10] he has grown up in. His attachment to his mother is still strong. His respect for the Church is so deep that he cannot take its rites lightly, though he is moved to reject them. With a tremendous effort, straining his willpower to the utmost, Stephen begins to disentangle himself. He sees Ireland as an "afterthought of Europe," suffering from paralysis. His crumbling home becomes but one of the aspects of his rotting country. His father, whose career he describes to his friend Cranly as follows: "A medical student, an oarsman, a tenor, an amateur actor, a shouting politician, a small landlord, a small investor, a drinker, a good fellow, a storyteller, somebody's secretary, something in the distillery, a taxgatherer, a bankrupt and at present a praiser of his own past," [11] appears a typical product or specimen of this once jolly, gay, and reckless but now godforsaken country, that would like to make time stop to perpetuate its own decaying reality in the face of a flourishing pulsating Europe advancing at giant's strides, just across the channel.

Stephen's preoccupations, his daring and freely expressed speculations, his determination to consider nobody but himself and to follow no rules or accepted patterns of behavior but those he himself imposes in accordance with the discipline to which an artist's mind should be subjected, make Stephen quite exceptionally egoistic. As a result he gets further removed from everybody. He is driven more and more into his own self, becoming gradually more isolated from life. Most revealing in this respect are the pages of *Stephen Hero*, only in part used for the final version of the *Portrait*. Written before its author had defined the artist as a God-like being who must withdraw from his own artifact, these pages give Stephen more body, more verisimilitude, more individuality as a character. His friendship with the boys of his age and his gradual alienation from them become more vivid. His own awareness of himself as a living being and the apprehension of Stephen as such by his fellows are more fully rendered in this manuscript. His friends' censure of his egoism, their resentment against his arrogant self-centeredness, are brought home more directly, together with his dangerous assumption of superiority.[12]

The difference between *Stephen Hero* and the *Portrait* is not only that it is more detailed and, in this simple sense, closer to natural reality. It is also more conventional in form. The author tells Stephen's story. Though both narratives are written in the third person, the earlier version gives us the direct, circumstantial story of the boy's formation, complete with descriptions of his appearance, the reactions of others to him, in short the usual direct and oblique fictional information, whereas in the *Portrait*, whatever we get to know has to come through Stephen's mind. In the purely technical sense it is one of the first modern psychological novels. The importance of the human mind, of our "sense of things,"[13] of consciousness, so central with James and Conrad, is here further explored.

The consequences are twofold. On the one hand, the reader gets to know Stephen's personal, internal existence more intimately. He goes with him through the successive stages of his growth, from a child reacting to reality with his senses, through his gradual emancipation from, and later his violent reaction against, the world he had so quietly and obediently accepted, until his final break with it. The external contours, however, seem to have got slightly blurred. Not once in the *Portrait* is the reader given either directly, through the author, or indirectly through any participants in the story, a description of the boy's outward appearance and manner. His portrait is like one of those surrealist paintings where the features of the face and the contours of the person are vaguely sketched to make them embrace the interior reality of the figure portrayed, visible through the surface sheen, transparent enough to allow the onlookers to see through

Another paradoxical consequence is that by placing the reader inside the boy's mind with the obvious intention of making him more individual and more specific, the author has made him less so. The reader is not only invited to identify himself with Stephen's mind; he cannot really understand or enjoy the book unless he does so. So Stephen is transformed from a specific person into a more general figure: not any young boy, but a young boy of a certain type—sophisticated, hypersensitive, proud, intellectual, with acute sense perceptions, especially of hearing. He has no intense individuality, and lacks the roundness of a fully dimensional character. By concentrating on the internal life of the boy, watching him through the prism of his mind, and consistently analysing his reactions to life, the author has somehow broken apart the completeness of the boy's individual being. We apprehend Stephen and the world he moves in as presences, we can hear him and the others, but we can hardly see him; we are not in a position to identify him as a complete individual personality. While in search of a more immediate reality, Joyce has drifted away from outward experience and sacrificed an element of objective firmness in the main character.

It is after sixteen, when he has decided to reject the offer to join the Jesuit order, that his personal development takes a specific, unusual direction. He has refused to be God's servant, a vocation that used to attract him and seemed for long the highest he could attain. Once he has in his revolt thrown the fetters of the Church away, the sense of freedom seems to go to his head. Stephen's revolt, rising from his disappointment in his father, spreads to embrace not only his country and its religion but God Himself. He must assume the role of God, become himself the rejected father figure, so that he may attempt to create a better world. His definition of different genres of literary art leads him on to the presumption of the godlike attributes of the artist; once the "mystery of aesthetic like that of material creation is accomplished . . . [the] artist, like the God of creation, remains within or behind or beyond or above his handi-work, invisible, refined out of existence, indifferent, paring his fingernails." [14] His theory of art, however, remains subjective and so idealistic and incomplete, since the self-created figure of the artist is its beginning and its end. It is thoroughly Nietzschean in its definition of art as "the human disposition of sensible or intelligible matter for an aesthetic end." [15]

Now that Stephen is to be an artist, his path is traced, the direction to be taken indicated. He becomes increasingly critical of his country and countrymen and, in accordance with his own theory, begins to drift away. He is alienated from his mother when he refuses to do his Easter duty and ridicules Church and creed. The obvious consequence is that he loses interest in everything his immediate surroundings can offer. He neglects his studies. By assuming a godlike attitude of superiority to everybody, he withdraws into himself, and loneliness begins "to close on him"—as Conrad put it in the case of Lord Jim.[16] He is no longer part of his milieu, he is above it. Thinking of his people he is preoccupied, again on Nietzschean lines, with the problem of how he could "hit their conscience or how cast his shadow over the imaginations of their daughters, before their squires begat upon them, that they might breed a race less ignoble than their own." [17] He soon reaches the point where he has either to grow out of his adolescent revolt and change into a different, a mature human being, or stubbornly persevere in it wherever it may take him. He takes this second alternative.

With a loud declaration, "I will not serve that in which I no longer believe, whether it call itself my home, my fatherland, or my church: and I will try to express myself in some mode of life or art as freely as I can and as wholly as I can, using for my defence the only arms I allow myself to use—silence, exile and cunning," [18] he decides to leave his country. He cannot live in the parochial atmosphere of Dublin, or share the fortune of his declining family with the humiliation and degradation that accompany it. He must assume the function he has assigned himself in life. With a most daring, pretentious, and—in a strict sense—impossible goal, "Welcome, O life! I go to encounter for the millionth time the reality of experience and to forge in the smithy of my soul the uncreated conscience of my race," [19] Stephen leaves his country.

From an extra sensitive and would-be meek child—the pattern is familiar—Stephen grows into a rebel. At eighteen or nineteen he has left everything behind, family, kin, and country. He has chosen exile and loneliness, in a world which by implication is malevolent, since he has to use "silence" and "cunning" in self-defence. He is deliberately separated from the rest of mankind in order to recreate it in conscience, in the conscious center of its being. Where such a separation from one's fellow men, such a dissociation from common reality, can lead one is all too well known to modern psychology. Persistence in such an attitude can lead to an alienation and ultimately a disintegration of one's personality. The attempt to reject reality, i.e. to deny it, and, by turning inward, create one's own reality, while ignoring the actual life flowing with the passage of time inside and outside oneself, leads to a denial of one's own reality, one's own personality, and finally to one's destruction. But Stephen has art to fix this negative tendency upon, this is his outlet. His art, breaking with all familiar conventions, absorbs the alienation that would otherwise—if persisted in—have taken place in his own mind.

In the case under consideration, given the book's autobiographical basis, may we be allowed to refer in our analysis of Stephen's character to what followed in the writer's career? The author himself never completely cut the umbilical cord that tied him to his offspring, never fully dissociated himself from the Stephen of his novels. This is probably why the figure of Stephen becomes less palpable, less physically present, as the *Portrait* proceeds.

The novel, concentrating on increasingly refined stages in the young artist's development, leaves the rest for the reader to create in his own imagination. Why should the reader guess at what followed in Stephen's life, why make conjectures as to where such an attitude, so clearly Joyce's own, might have taken Stephen, if he has the novelist's career itself to show what it led to? Through the Stephen of the *Portrait* but equally through the author's subsequent creations, we are given an especially revealing insight into the fortunes of the human figure and the crisis in human values in the critical period that sets in with the outbreak of the First World War and continues through the interwar period.

An uncompromisingly honest attempt to find what life and reality mean to modern man and what values one might live by in a world whose all-accepted truths had proved false, led Joyce to the act of rebellion and separation that he creates as a living experience in Stephen's mind, and to the heroic and probably thankless task of creating a racial "conscience" for the people he had broken away from, showing them what they are and reminding them of what they should be. It is life's little irony that James Joyce, who in the figure of his Stephen left Ireland with such a decisive gesture of rejection, should have continued to live in it, live with it in his mind, all his remaining life. Having rejected the temporal reality of Ireland, the artist recreates it outside the flow of time, fixed in a past moment for all eternity. His search for reality becomes a psychoanalysis of his own memory. He collects tram tickets, posters, fans, odds and ends that belong to that one moment, June 16, 1904, as though by arranging these relics in a pattern of restored consciousness, he might also restore them to life. In *Ulysses* time is frozen and the characters are immobilized, arrested, given as changeless. They are not dramatically alive; they *stand*, each, for one facet of human character or, better, for types of the human personality. We can hear them, we can merge with their stream of thought, but we can hardly see them. We live their day in Dublin but we cannot identify them as individuals.

Already in *Ulysses* Joyce is at times on the point of taking his last, most fatal leap, that of alienating the reader—his strongest remaining link with reality—by exercising too great a freedom in his subjective use of language. Communication through language exists for better or worse on the conscious level. By attempting to follow the internal flow of thought on a level below articulate speech, Joyce has made his great characters in *Ulysses* more fluid but at the same time less continuous, less identifiable as living beings in the flow of time. Adhering too strictly to the subjective principle and using as little as possible the organizing prerogative of the omniscient author, he has not only made the book too long and taxing to read for the story it contains, but has deprived it of dramatic tension and episodic clarity. This does not seem to have bothered him because he himself, lonely exile in actual fact and god of creation in his own imagination, had all the patience necessary for laboring through his book, however saturated it became with scholastic divagations and all the endless circumlocutions of the catechising scholar.

All this, however, still could be contained within the broad confines of fiction. There is a story and a moral meaning, which can be deciphered. But Joyce could not stop there. In order to realize the plan announced in the *Portrait* and reach his ultimate artistic goal, he must go further into the sphere of the unconscious. Here Joyce's lot becomes even more typical of a pioneer generation swept off their feet by the early glimpse into the chaos of the unconscious mind. Fearlessly exploring for themselves, they went ahead of science in their anticipation of the further discoveries hinted at in their texts. Once entranced by the vastness of the unconscious, they did not seem able to turn back to reality and create in living characters a synthesis of both subjective experience and the objective contingent reality of individual life.

By trying to create in *Finnegans Wake* the language of the unconscious—which does not form a normative system of sounds, words, communicable and intelligible, since the human personality on the unconscious level does not exist as a separate individual—Joyce destroyed or rather disintegrated the accepted linguistic forms. Out of the separated parts of words he formed new entities, using for this monstruous invented language many different European and non-European sources. At this stage of his life and career, his psychology of exile had made him practically impervious to human contact. He completely disregarded his potential reader. Yet somewhere below the surface he probably knew that he was trying to do the impossible. He knew that our unity, our identity and continuity as active beings, were lost when we were on the unconscious level, asleep. So he made his Earwicker sleep or rather dream, in order to liberate himself from all restriction. This allowed him to create freely and with utmost care the linguistic riot of *Finnegans Wake*. At the same time he reached far out beyond his own "racial conscience" for support. The structure of *Finnegans Wake*, without which he could hardly have persisted in this lonely task through seventeen years of his life, was provided by old Indo-European myths, which are given the status of sacred rituals. Born and bred in the ritualistic environment of home, schooling, and Church, he found in the formally rejected patterns of ritual by which he was entranced in adolescence all the support he needed to persevere in his ultimate alienation from the world while creating his unintelligible *Finnegans Wake*, the most brilliant and masterly failure literature has ever known.

All this that may seem mere conjecture is suggested by Joyce himself, in his projection of Stephen in the *Portrait*. "In vague sacrificial or sacramental acts alone his will seemed drawn to go forth to encounter reality: and it was partly the absence of an appointed rite which had always constrained him to inaction whether he had allowed silence to cover his anger or pride or had suffered only an embrace he longed to give." [20] Without the ritualistic mythological stories to mark his way, Joyce could hardly have persisted in his titanic effort, cutting himself completely off from his fellow men apart from an occasional kindred spirit or enthusiastic scholar, or—and this would not have pleased Joyce—from psychoanalysts determined to trace in his text the pattern of some specific mental aberration in the author's personality. And yet all the time, his acute intelligence and perspicacity seemed to be fully alive. Deep in his being he must have been aware of the impossibility of his struggle. One of the more haunting metaphors in *Finnegans Wake* seems to indicate it: "Fieluhr? Filou! What age is at? It saon is late. 'Tis endless now seene eye or erewone last saw Waterhouse's clogh. They took it asunder, I hurd thum sigh. When will they reassemble it?" [21]

This is where we may assume Stephen's development in the *Portrait*, crowned by his final decision and turning inward upon his own isolated consciousness, would have led him. In *Finnegans Wake* the dreamer asks what time it is—because time, the medium of life the author has chosen to disregard, seems to dog his steps. He is haunted by the vision of a dismantled clock that nobody can put together again. Since he has assumed the role of the "God of creation" he should be able to create a complete human figure, but he could not do so. He could analyse, fragmentize, break up man and reality into countless splinters, atomize them, but he could never put them together again. However carefully he might have assembled the bits and pieces, the relics and symbols of life, contained in the magic of myths, he could not breathe life into them. His vision of the future strikes one as that of a return to a planet getting cold again, to the humanless world of rock and stone of T. S. Eliot's *Waste Land*.[22] Life has stopped, sounds die, everything seems to revert to stone alongside the flowing river, whose very flow, symbol of time, seems to contradict the efforts of the artist: "Night now! Tell me, tell me, tell me, elm! Night night! Telmetale of stem or stone. Beside the rivering waters of, hither and thithering waters of. Night!" [23]

In his persistent search for a greater, internal reality, Joyce, more grandly than any other artist of his generation, lost his way. While blundering through the unmapped area of the unconscious he finally landed in a wasteland from which life was gradually departing, our planet becoming lifeless again. No poet seems to have found a more vivid metaphor for the dead end to which his lonely quest has led him than James Joyce in his appeal to the night to tell him the tale of "stem or stone." [24]

4

Clarissa Dalloway

> Death was defiance. Death was an attempt to communicate;
> people feeling the impossibility of reaching the centre which,
> mystically, evaded them; closeness drew apart; rapture faded,
> one was alone. There was an embrace in death.[1]

At the time Virginia Woolf was writing *Mrs. Dalloway*
she had consciously taken a stand towards literature, the
novel in particular. In her criticism of the realistic novel
of her contemporaries—Bennett, Wells, Galsworthy, the
materialists, as she called them—she had formulated her
own conception of character in fiction. She shared with
them, Bennett specially, the idea that it was the building
of character that mattered most. Unlike traditional realistic novelists, however, she equated the human personality with the mind. She claimed that it is the mind that
the novelist is concerned with and that everything else is
secondary to one all-important end—that of elucidating
the working, the inner functioning, of the mind. If one
takes her pronouncement on what reality consists of, the
by now classical passage on the working of an ordinary
mind on an ordinary day, as a key to her novels, one
comes to the conclusion that it is in *Mrs. Dalloway* that
Virginia Woolf has most fully and most successfully
applied the technique resulting from her attitude to
reality.

If one assumes that it is the mind and the mind alone
that matters, and that the only mind one can really see
into is one's own, then the character into which the
author has poured most of himself will be the most fully
created, the most authentic. It will, however, inevitably
be most closely associated with, if not inseparable from,
its creator. Also, the personal, subjective apprehension of

life, of one's own existence and experience is nowhere so completely satisfying as in tracing the chief character's discovery of itself, in the case of Clarissa Dalloway. In this, more consistently than in any other of her novels, Virginia Woolf relies upon the subjective, stream of consciousness technique to reveal the character from the inside. She confines the action of the novel to one day, so that the pace of apprehension comes as close as possible to the pace of the characters' interior flow of consciousness. With the time sequence of the novel approximating the reader's own experience of time, the reader can respond to whatever Clarissa's consciousness, her mind, may gather, react to, engage in association with, or reject.

The process going in the novel's central consciousness is highly selective. Clarissa's mind is the foremost of a number of mirrors reflecting what Virginia Woolf thought worth registering in human existence. In this mirror she sees her own reflection, together with the reflections thrown back by the minds of the other protagonists. By this means we see her both as she appears to her own consciousness and as she appears to others when, so to speak, she is off her guard. Both points of view contribute to the elucidation of her character, the fullest confession of Virginia Woolf's conception of human personality. *Mrs. Dalloway* is the author's most immediate statement of what the life of the self—now open arena, now circumscribed prison—really is, and of what, within the confines of one's own personality and the social ambience one is born to, can be done with one's own existence.

We get to know Mrs. Dalloway by sharing with her the experiences of one day in her life. It is a day on which she gives one of her parties. Mrs. Dalloway is a woman of the world, a well-known hostess in whose house even prime ministers may be seen. Such an event in her life makes her think of everything that has preceded, that has led up to it. Her glance also goes forward to what still remains. Much of her life is already behind her, even if she may not be ready to admit that the best part of it is gone. She makes the last preparations for the party. She buys flowers, sees people, meets some old friends, looks to the arrangements at home. Her mind is concentrated on the great event to take place in the evening, and yet all the time other things and people, flowing in and out of her life, arrest her attention—friends from childhood; her daughter and the instructress she loathes; her husband, invited to a lunch by a distinguished dowager who seems to ignore Clarissa; her maid. As the evening draws on and the lights grow dim, her green dress has been repaired and she is ready, and the party takes place. It is a glittering party of the highest distinction. Clarissa, the "perfect hostess," [2] enjoys one of the moments in which her life seems to reach a culmination. And then, at the party, another destiny, which like an accompanying motif has been running parallel with hers, interferes. Death is mentioned, death "in the middle of . . . [her] party." [3] Clarissa suffers a shock that leads to a moment of recognition but fortunately stops short of the climax. She rejoins the guests, the party is a success. Another great day of her life has fulfilled her expectations. She can continue, for life has a "way of adding day to day." [4]

"Mrs. Dalloway said she would buy the flowers herself." [5] As she goes out, on a fresh June morning, she is reminded of her youth, the sensation she had listening to the noises in the house that accompany the preparations for a reception in the evening. "What a lark! What a plunge! For so it had always seemed to her when . . . she had burst open the French windows and plunged at Bourton into the open air." [6] She loves the mist gathering on the branches of the trees, the haziness of a London morning. The streets are crowded with people who don't know each other and yet all contribute to what

London is, a murmuring sea carrying in its tides countless lives. In its color, noise, atmosphere, it symbolizes
the life of a community to which Clarissa feels happy
and proud to belong. Reminiscences of youth and its
glamor evoked by the excitement of the forthcoming
evening, when she will again be the centre of a gathering
of people she alone has created, confront Clarissa with
an idea of her entire life. The deeply buried uncertainty
as to whether life has fulfilled the promise her youth had
held breaks through the gaiety roused by the day and the
always inspiring vitality of London.

> Did it matter then, she asked herself, walking towards
> Bond Street, did it matter that she must inevitably cease
> completely; all this must go on without her; did she resent
> it; or did it not become consoling to believe that death
> ended absolutely? but that somehow in the streets of
> London, on the ebb and flow of things, here, there, she
> survived.[7]

Clarissa has grown into Mrs. Dalloway, lady of the
world, to whose party people think it a distinction to be
invited. From a passionate, susceptible young girl she has
developed into a "perfect hostess." Used to the discussion of literature, poetry, specific problems of human
conduct, she was fairly ignorant of the larger social problems that never penetrated the secluded domestic world
of the upper classes in the eighties. The mention of sex
would have made her blush. And yet she could accept
and cherish the friendship of Sally Seton, an unconventional frank girl who spoke her mind directly, hated
social superiority, jeered at snobbery, and had once
shocked the entire household at Bourton by walking
stark naked from the bathroom. Clarissa fell in love with
her for her vitality and outspokenness, the freedom she
herself could not assume but admired in others. The fact
that Sally smoked cigars and rode on a bicycle on the
parapet, that she had come from a disrupted home of
parents who quarrelled, all this but drew Clarissa closer
to her. It was only in middle age that conventionality,

and a certain social rigidity and narrowmindedness, had closed in on Clarissa. In youth she had pitted her mind against that of Peter Walsh. Did she love him or not?— that remains a question with her. He had loved her. But Clarissa was afraid of intensity. She could not stand his constant questioning, his appeal to be in her mind all the time and share everything. He reproached her for snobbery, called her timid, hard, arrogant, unimaginative, prudish, accused her of the "death of the soul." [8] She could not help it. There was something in her to which she could allow access to nobody. Was it, as the author hints, the result of the shock of her sister's tragic death, killed by a falling tree under Clarissa's eyes? Whatever the cause, she fled from Peter's passionate love into the arms of the unimaginative Richard Dalloway. With him she would be able to exercise what Peter conceded as her ability, to entertain, to keep a kind of *salon*, to "carry things through." [9]

But what has this ability won for her? What is it her entire life consists in, or rather what has it been reduced to? What has she made of it? These are the questions Clarissa puts to herself, but she can just as little answer them as she can see into herself. The only thing she discovers raging in her, that makes her feel fully, if maliciously, alive, is hatred for Miss Kilman, the repulsive instructress who seems to have got hold of her daughter and is now taking her away from her mother.

> It rasped her, though, to have stirring about in her this brutal monster! to hear twigs cracking and feel hooves planted down in the depths of that leaf-encumbered forest, the soul; never to be content quite, or quite secure, for at any moment the brute would be stirring, this hatred, which, especially since her illness, had power to make her feel scraped, hurt in her spine; gave her physical pain, and made all pleasure in beauty, in friendship, in being well, in being loved and making her home delightful rock, quiver, and bend as if indeed there were a monster grubbing at the roots, as if the whole panoply of content were nothing but self love! this hatred! [10]

Clarissa is horrified at this dark, destructive passion in-side her, so far beneath the demeanor of the perfect hostess, the role she has successfully performed so far. An unavowed bitterness of frustration seems to have emerged during her illness, at a time when conscious controls had relaxed. She is shocked, she cannot account for the loathing she feels for the poor, ugly, arrogant, and unpleasant Miss Kilman—she, who always tries so hard to be "kind to people," [11] and thinks she really is kind.

Clarissa tries to understand what made her choose Richard Dalloway instead of Peter Walsh, for whom she might, as it seems to her now at fifty-two, have devel-oped a passion. She realizes that it was her fear of life—she cannot see it is really a fear of herself—that has made her decide for the safety and protection of a dull, opaque man rather than for the restless, passionate Peter with his vivid, exalted perception of things, his full-hearted participation in life. Fear and hatred is all she can find in herself as governing her life and awakening her to existence. Richard was more convenient. He could protect her from "the heat of the day." He did not see into her, as had Peter. In Richard's eyes she saw herself reflected just as she wished to believe she really was. He saw her as she presented herself to him.

Clarissa tried so hard to be loved and to establish herself in other people's inclination. Her inability to break through the defenses of the unattractive and vin-dictive Miss Kilman irritates her all the more when Miss Kilman is impervious to Clarissa's unconscious efforts to charm her and win her over. Richard loved her and she could make herself believe that she loved him. Perhaps she gave him as much affection as she could ever give anybody, an affection so applied as to get in return a full and absolute adoration, a devotion that will never for a moment look upon her critically, never come to the point of seeing through her. With him she was safe. She could securely exist only on the glittering surface of things where people moved and combined like figures in a classical ballet where no human contact was allowed, the figures and the arabesques excluding all communication.

Peter was different. He was involved in life and people. He saw through shams and pretenses. Just because he was attracted to her when she still considered the possibility of giving herself away, when she loved to plunge into the freshness of a summer morning in the country at Bourton, he would have broken through the integuments guarding her inner being. But this she could not allow. For what was there in her but a chaos of fear and hatred? She could only continue to act in the sham world of appearances if she left the void inside her untouched, pretended that it did not exist. Now that Peter is back after so many years she again feels that she likes him, but she is just as certain that she was right in refusing him. Yet his confession of love for another woman upsets her. It makes her send him a note with just one sentence: "Heavenly to see you." [12] It is not only the jealousy that survives love, a kind of female vanity, that prompts her to do so, nor is it only a dog-in-the-manger selfishness and greed; it is again her fear of a confrontation with herself. Peter's ability to get away from her and shake off her influence shatters the little self-confidence, the precarious image of her own success with her life, with which she faces her world.

Richard is safe. He is blissfully happy with her and does not interfere. He has never tried to take possession of her thoughts, her emotions, her entire being. She wants to be cherished, not passionately loved, not challenged to a new existence. Since she can give nothing, love with her cannot be communication and exchange. She could only take, she could not give. Therefore she felt that passionate love could only devour her as she was. She has made a whole theory of the beauty of solitude. Complete communion should not be allowed to enter even the most intimate relationship between man and wife. "And there is a dignity in people; a solitude; even between husband and wife a gulf; and that one must respect, thought Clarissa, watching him open the door; for one would not part with it oneself, or take it, against his will, from one's husband, without losing one's independence, one's self-respect—something, after all, priceless." [13]

Clarissa clings to her apartness, her solitude, her self-imposed isolation. She wants to be left alone and to leave everybody else alone. There will be no passion, no fervent involvement anywhere for her. She loathes causes, whether religious or political, anything that engages a full-hearted participation. She is afraid of every strong feeling or conviction that would immerse her in life. "Love destroyed too. Everything that was fine, everything that was true went. Take Peter Walsh now. There was a man, charming, clever, with ideas about everything . . . Think of Peter in love—he came to see her after all these years, and what did he talk about? Himself. Horrible passion! she thought. Degrading passion!" [14]

Her daughter Elizabeth is likewise kept at a distance. Clarissa must feel she has absolute sway over her. Elizabeth, too, must move in the glory of her mother's brilliance. She cannot be permitted to get away and build her own life, for if Clarissa's absolute supremacy in her artificial world of family and high life society is challenged, she is lost. She knows that both her husband and her daughter would have been much happier in the country, on a farm, but she needs crowds of smart people; she must move in the leading circles, be surrounded by prominent figures, have the adulation of strangers, who will never come close enough to see through her. Alone in the country with nobody to supply her with a shining reflection of herself as a brilliant woman of the world, she would dissolve and disappear. She has not built her own life, her own personality; she has refused her own being access into the shell of the well-groomed Mrs. Dalloway. She must cling to this flattering reflection of herself for this has become her only reality. Those who would deprive her of it—Peter Walsh, Sally Seton—are finally her enemies. They are dangerous, they

would take away from her the security she has been
carefully building all the long empty years, "adding day
to day," [15] just to be able to survive.

Her diffidence at the opening of the party comes
partly from her awareness of Peter's critical eye. He had
despised this worldliness in her, as had Sally, who had
begged him to save Clarissa from the gentleman that
would make "a mere hostess of her." [16] But as people
assemble she begins to feel surer. She knows that Peter
and Sally were wrong. Her parties mean something essential to her. It is life to her bringing together people
from different ends of London, who know nothing about
each other's existence: "it was an offering; to combine,
to create; but to whom? An offering for the sake of
offering, perhaps. Anyhow, it was her gift. Nothing else
had she of the slightest importance; could not think,
write, even play the piano." [17] But the emptiness of it all,
that she herself cannot but perceive, brings into her
mind the undercurrent of her thoughts and of her entire
existence, her constant fear of death. "After that, how
unbelievable death was!—that it must end; and no one
in the whole world would know she had loved it all." [18]

The party reaches its high-water mark:

> Clarissa escorted her Prime Minister down the room,
> prancing, sparkling, with the stateliness of her grey hair
> . . . Lolloping on the waves and braiding her tresses she
> seemed, having that gift still; to be; to exist; to sum it all
> up in the moment as she passed; turned, caught her scarf
> in some other woman's dress, unhitched it, laughed, all
> with the most perfect ease and air of a creature floating in
> its element.[19]

And then, out of the blue, the famous Doctor Bradshaw and his wife bring the news of a young man who
has killed himself. This immediately strikes a chord in
Clarissa's being: "in the middle of my party, here's
death, she thought." [20] The whole shimmering world
suddenly dissolves as though it had been made of soap
bubbles. From beneath her shallow existence, her death

in life comes to the surface. She identifies herself with the young man. Her intuition, one of the gifts Peter admired most in her, makes her realize that he had chosen death to avoid compromising with life, while she "had once thrown a shilling into the Serpentine, never anything more." [21] She has had the kind of life she could have without plunging into it unreservedly and yet there was a thing "that mattered; a thing, wreathed about with chatter, defaced, obscured in her own life, let drop every day in corruption, lies, chatter. This he had preserved." [22] And with all that how lonely she is. Death seems the only escape from one's closed-in self, an escape into a community beyond consciousness. For a twinkle of a moment she envies Septimus Warren Smith.

But a simple vitality prevails. She admits her incapacity to handle her own life. She could never walk serenely with it. The young man's death seems to be *her* disaster, *her* disgrace, yet she is alive. Even the slow ebbing monotony of her own existence seems better than death. She has looked for a moment into the abyss of her own darkness. This unknown young man's death, the fact that he had thrown all this away, "made her feel the beauty; made her feel the fun" of life. She is herself again. She can rejoin the guests: "she must go back. She must assemble." [23] What is it she must assemble?

Within the period of one day the reader is initiated into the whole life of Clarissa Dalloway and given access into her personality. In the manner of the modern psychological novel, the focus is always in the minds of the characters, now one, now another. Objective information seems to be given only about characters in peripheral roles. No information is directly supplied in the author's voice. Everything is presented obliquely and subjectively, the inward experience of different people flowing in and out of each other's lives, but all contributing primarily to the full evocation of the main character, Clarissa. She herself is the chief source of information about herself, but without the reflection we have of her in the minds of the others she could hardly have been given in the round. We see her just as people round her see her: "A charming woman, Scrope Purvis thought her [knowing her as one does know people who live next door to one in Westminster]; a touch of the bird about her, of the jay, blue-green, light, vivacious, though she was over fifty, and grown very white since her illness. There she perched, never seeing him, waiting to cross, very upright." [24] Chance passersby together with people who know her better throw light on her now from that angle, now from this. From various impressions in the minds of different persons Clarissa Dalloway forms into a solid figure. She seems to belong to herself just as much as to all those who take part in her life in the visually vivid, but, refracted as it always is in the minds of others, never quite solid enough world of Virginia Woolf's invention.

Clarissa's version of herself is revealing in spite of her extraordinary ability to impose her own interpretation on things and ignore what she is loath to face. She still sees herself as the young girl in white walking on the terrace at Bourton. She had liked to think of herself as good and kind, and as spreading out her personality to include the whole world she cares for. But this view of her, indeed all that is most valuable and lastingly important about her, is offered us by Peter Walsh. Peter criticizes her more sharply than anybody, but he knows her more intimately, too. He understood her, her unused and never to be probed potentialities, her intuitive knowledge of things and peoples: "she felt herself everywhere; not 'here, here, here'; and she tapped the back of the seat; but everywhere. She waved her hand, going up Shaftsbury Avenue. She was all that. So that to know her, or any one, one must seek out the people who completed them; even the places." [25] From her he learned to "see round things." [26] He knew her self-centred self-love, her snobbery, the cruelty to her social inferiors that Clarissa herself was not aware of and would not have admitted. He understood that things had changed radically between 1918 and 1923 and that her time and place were in the past. Then there was that "horror of death" which she had to keep at bay all her life, and she was a nonbeliever; she had nothing, nobody but herself, to fall back upon. She made up almost

> a transcendental theory, which, with her horror of death, allowed her to believe, or say that she believed [for all her scepticism], that since our apparitions, the part of us which appears, are so momentary compared with the other, the unseen part of us, which spreads wide, the unseen might survive, be recovered somehow attached to this person or that, or even haunting certain places after death . . . perhaps—perhaps.[27]

And yet with all her inward sensibility and kindness, the worldly superficial Clarissa carries the day. At her reception Peter sees her "at her worst—effusive, insincere." [28] Unlike Peter, Richard does not really understand her. He feels that she needs protection and he is too glad to give it to her. Her attachment to her husband is not passionate. She is too preoccupied with herself to think of him, or of anybody else, as a separate being. Her daughter has not, as it seems, roused any profound motherhood in her. Clarissa is lonely. She has avoided strong feelings. She has built powerful ramparts between herself and the world so that she could hide behind them.

But with Clarissa Virginia Woolf had something more to convey than just this. In *Mrs. Dalloway*, whether or not she herself was aware of it, she had to get the ghost by the throat, to externalize and so rid herself of her own fear of life and her horror of death, so that she might survive and continue. Without any obvious narrative logic she introduces a parallel life that runs all the time like a subterranean stream under the firm ground of the novel's outward show of characters and events. Septimus Warren Smith is a projection of that dark invisible side of the luminous London hostess. Without any of her dodges and subterfuges he goes straight to his doom. Their lives do not meet, but their stories, their images, merge.

Bringing them together, making their paths tangentially touch or even cross, was no special problem for an author whose stream of consciousness technique, exacting and limiting on the one hand, gives great freedom of movement on the other. Septimus Warren Smith's fate is brought home to Clarissa before the end of her day, at the moment of her apogee, her triumph, precisely when the fragile human self is most liable to fall from the heights it has scaled. Septimus had suppressed his natural reaction to the violent death of his friend Evans, killed by a bomb explosion at his side in the war; had refused to face his own feelings. He was himself surprised at his equanimity and self-control. Then this *Gleichgultigkeit*,[29] like an infection, spread all over his being. He began to fear his indifference. To save himself he acted as Clarissa had done. He married a gay and simple Italian girl in the hope that her reassuring presence might help him to break through his own loneliness. He thought he could lean against her and so retain his sanity. But his case is worse, and the corrosive process goes on. Panic at his inability to feel makes him turn to books. But everywhere, in Shakespeare, Dante, Aeschylus, he finds hatred, despair, loathing of life. The destructive urge in him is unleashed, and comes out into the open.

His wife Lucrezia would like to help him, and thinks that having a child, a son, will reassure him. But he is opposed: "One cannot bring children into a world like this. One cannot perpetuate suffering, or increase the breed of these lustful animals, who have no lasting emotions, but only whims and vanities, eddying them now this way, now that." [30] Septimus tries to fight these nightmares. He fails, and he gives in, though "nothing whatever [is] the matter, except the sin for which human nature had condemned him to death; that he did not feel." [31] The only way out is suicide. The simpleminded Dr. Holmes cannot help him, but seems rather to have won Rezia over and taken her away from him. Septimus feels deserted. He sinks into profound isolation. He must battle in his own timeless world with the spectres of the past, and talk aloud with Evans. The world of doctors closes in on him, the inept Dr. Holmes, the cold smooth Sir William Bradshaw, and his resistence breaks. It is "human nature" itself that is against him—"the repulsive brute, with the blood-red nostrils" [32]—and the only escape is death. Septimus throws himself through the window.

This undercurrent in the novel's action is obviously relevant to the reader's understanding of Clarissa. How else could Virginia Woolf have explained Clarissa's suppressed awareness of her own loneliness; how could she have found words, or an adequate metaphor, for her pessimistic belief that since life refuses communication there is "an embrace in death"? [33] Septimus has given in; Clarissa has not. She has had her dark vision; for a twinkling of a second she had seen into her own subterfuges, but then she recovered control over herself. Her unbroken vitality had come to her aid. No more than Septimus could she help being what she was: "there was the terror; the overwhelming incapacity, one's parents giving it into one's hands, this life, to be lived to the end, to be walked with serenely; there was in the depths of her heart an awful fear." [34] She sees herself clearly enough: "She had schemed; she had pilfered. She was never wholly admirable. She had wanted success . . . And once she had walked on the terrace at Bourton." [35] The vision of her untainted youth rouses her from her hallucinations. She is back in the midst of all this, alive: he is dead. Her very survival is her triumph.

Clarissa Dalloway is an offspring of the cultivated upper classes, the English gentry, possessed, within her sphere, of a keen mind, a refined sensibility, a penetrating intuition, an imagination that responds to nature, flowers, trees, the atmosphere at Bourton, the mood of London. She is sentimental—but is she kind? Her understanding stops on the frontiers of her world, that of her social equals. She does not try to enter into the minds and lives of people outside it, she is condescending to them, appreciative of the effort they make to please her, treating them like servants. If they are poor, unkempt, dirty, deformed, she has nothing but loathing for them. They rouse in her no compassion; rather, they bring out her horror of life that is there immediately under the surface. Whether or not it was caused by the shock suffered in her childhood, this horror makes her withdraw into herself, into her own locked-up feelings. It has not allowed her to give herself away either to the man she loved, Peter, or to anybody or anything else, husband, daughter, "cause," or interest. Is it only fear of life? Is it not just as much a fear of herself, of the life going on inside her? She dares not face the "cosmos" outside because she dreads the chaos inside her. She ignores what Peter calls the "soul": "our self, who fish-like inhabits deep seas and plies among obscurities treading her way between the boles of giant weeds, over sun-flickered spaces and on and on into gloom, cold, deep, inscrutable." [36]

To compensate for the suppression of her human and womanly inclinations, she cultivates her *self*, her egoism, her snobbery. With the years, rigidity turns into conventionality, social superiority into intolerance. She becomes increasingly lonely. The only outlet are her parties. They not only flatter her worldliness, her vanity; they provide vitality, the bustle of life. They fill the emptiness, the vacuum which her resistance to feeling and to involvement with life and people has allowed to grow inside her. The war-shattered world that is changing round her makes her position even more precarious. She is no longer as secure in her superior social position as she used to be, no longer as fully protected from the things in life she cannot face. Form is no longer kept as it used to be. Everything, including sex, is discussed in public. Even in her own secluded world Clarissa is threatened. She cannot find support in religion, having inherited only agnosticism from her parents. She cannot find any metaphysical basis for her life. And yet she must keep the surface intact. She cannot allow the darkness underneath to pierce through this surface, under attack now from all sides.

The troubled world would see things as they are, wrench the mask of all shams, unveil the unrest that has been accumulating within the *self* and would come up now. Time flows on. Most of Clarissa's life is already gone and she still stands on the stairs, all in white, playing her role, trying to delude not only the others, as she has managed to do, but herself; to project the glamor of her vanished youth into all eternity. She cannot accept the passage of time in an existence devoid of content. Her panic of life and terror of death increase. She is imprisoned in herself: "for what can one know even of the people one lives with every day? . . . Are we not all prisoners?" [37] The *self*, where all the suffering is centered, prevents us from communicating. Life is not what it was supposed to be. It is a prison, and liberation comes once we have shaken it off: "Death was defiance. Death was an attempt to communicate; people feeling the impossibility of reaching the centre which, mystically, evaded them; closeness drew apart; rapture faded, one was alone. There was an embrace in death." [38] So death is the one answer. If you reject life what are you left with but death? Clarissa's whole attitude to life led to its denial and ultimately to her own destruction, to death, as the only solution.

5

Tony Last

*I will show you something different from either
Your shadow at morning striding behind you
Or your shadow at evening rising to meet you;
I will show you fear in a handful of dust.*

The Waste Land [1]

A novelist whose attitude to life is best summed up in his statement that "nothing matters except the fact that nothing matters" could hardly offer the kind of character this essay is in search of. The figures that come to mind when one thinks of the world of Evelyn Waugh's novels are almost invariably comic caricatures, fixed one and all and incapable of development and change. They illustrate accurately enough one or two prominent features of the human make-up, but the profounder reality they represent is a certain attitude to man that expresses a whole era of history and that perhaps still prevails, a debasing attitude to which many of Waugh's generation [and not only the worst] succumbed. The spectacle is of performing circus animals; so Waugh himself described the behavior of characters in fiction.

In one novel, however, of his early and best period, *A Handful of Dust* [1934], the spectacle takes on a more general and objective truthfulness, and one is left with something more than the sense of debasement and frustration that normally follows one's exposure to the author's cynical wit. Reading this novel in the thirties, one felt a painful apprehension that this was not an isolated or special case, and that one's sympathy for Tony Last, different in kind from one's usual reaction to Waugh's characters, was sympathy for a condition of human life that typified the modern age. To look back at *Handful of Dust* from our present perspective is to discover that Tony Last's fate seems more than ever representative of what was happening to people who, losing control of their own lives, were being converted into performing puppets and were realizing too late what had been wasted and irretrievably lost. It is this atmosphere of waste and futility, of impotence and degradation, the inner quality of a whole era, that makes Tony Last the author's most sympathetic and most living character, the one who cannot be subsumed among the circus animals.

One's pity for Tony Last is pity for all those who, through passive participation in their own lives, have brought such a destiny upon themselves. He is not only the very picture of the helpless man, easy prey of any of the retrograde terrorist regimes of the time. He naïvely meets halfway whatever comes along. Unsure of his power or right to discriminate between good and evil, he is not prepared to resist evil before he is completely engulfed by it. Very much a thirties' figure, he seems also to anticipate the utterly resourceless character who materialized in the comedies of the absurd, most articulately in Beckett's *Waiting for Godot*, after the Second World War. He is more deeply representative of the attitudes and conditions of our time than any character in Evelyn Waugh's own later work. For with the coming of the war—and the change can be seen in *Brideshead Revisited* of 1945—Waugh turned to the past to find answers and consolations that neither the present nor the future seemed to offer. The characters of *Brideshead Revisited* and the later novels are artificial and peripheral, contrived to support the author's desperate determination to believe that the future could lie in a return to the past and its values; as such, they cannot embody a reaction to a common stock of living experience in the same way as Tony Last. To choose from his work one of these later characters rather than the most authentic and universally valid creation of his prime would not only be irrelevant to the purposes of the present essay but unfair to the novelist himself.

Tony Last is the offspring of an old aristocratic family. He lives with his wife, Brenda, and his seven-year-old son, John Andrew, in Hetton Abbey, "formerly one of the notable houses of the country . . . entirely rebuilt in 1864 in the Gothic style . . . now devoid of interest."[2] Tony's greatest and most lasting devotion goes to this house. He dotes on his wife and loves his son, but everything and everybody, himself and those dependent on or attached to him, are subject to his primary interest in life, Hetton. Of comfortable means but obliged to live a restricted life until the death duties are paid, Tony takes it for granted that his beautiful young wife should understand and share his attachment and so comply without resentment to the tedium of country life, the strict economizing imposed by the costs of living at Hetton. But for the sake of what? Tony never asks this question. Driven by boredom, aided by chance circumstance, Brenda drifts into dissolute London life. She engages in an affair with the good-for-nothing young social opportunist, John Beaver. After the accidental death of her son, John Andrew, she decides to separate. She leaves the pseudo-Gothic castle, embodiment of the failure of the married life, something like a prison to her. Tony is on the point of giving her a divorce on fair terms when her brother Reggie interferes, persuading her to demand an alimony which would entail selling Hetton. Tony refuses to give her a divorce. But with nothing to assuage the desolation of his life in an incomprehensible world, he joins an explorer bound on digging out a city in the jungle of Brazil, and never comes back again. Brenda marries Jock Grant-Menzies. Hetton goes to the impoverished Lasts, closest of kin. A memorial is erected on the gravel in front of the house, "a plain monolith of local stone," inscribed:

ANTHONY LAST OF HETTON

EXPLORER

Born at Hetton, 1902
Died in Brazil, 1934 [3]

Tony Last leads a contented life with his wife and son in
Hetton. He goes about his daily duties on the estate, and
he keeps the accounts carefully, for the money that goes
into keeping the Gothic house in repair and running
however modest a life there swallows up all his revenue.
The first two years of his married life were different.
Before his father died he and Brenda lived a gay life in
London. But after he had taken over the family estate
life had changed. There are fewer and fewer parties in
Hetton; guests do not often come. Tony likes it that
way. It never occurs to him that his wife might think it
monotonous. It is enough that life at Hetton continues
and that John Andrew grows up there—in the care, as it
works out, of Nanny and the stud-groom, Ben. Brenda
has nothing to do, but think of her diet. There is an
occasional visit to London, a rare—and dull—party at
Hetton. Appearances are kept. Tony is content to assume that everything is for the best. More often than
before his wife prefers to be left alone, but he does not
attach any importance to this. When she takes to going
to London more often and staying there longer he feels
deserted, but does not ask questions. He even accedes to
her taking a flat in London and accepts her overt lie that
she is studying economics and so must spend most of her
time in town. He gets annoyed when his son, uninhibited by breeding and manners, asks questions after
Tony's fruitless visit to his mother:

"Hullo, daddy, had a good time in London? You didn't
mind me coming to the station did you? I *made* nanny let
me."

"Very pleased to see you, John!"

"How was mummy?"

"She sounded very well, I didn't see her."

"But you *said* you were going to see her."

"Yes, I thought I was, but I turned out to be wrong. I talked to her several times on the telephone."

"But you can telephone her from here, can't you, daddy? Why did you go all the way to London to telephone to her? . . . *Why*, daddy?"

"It would take too long to explain."

"Well, tell me some of it . . . *Why*, daddy?"

"Look here I'm tired. If you don't stop asking questions I shan't let you ever come and meet the trains again."

John Andrew's face began to pucker. "I thought you'd *like* me to come and meet you."

"If you cry I shall put you in front with Dawson. It's absurd to cry at your age."

"I'd *sooner* go in front with Dawson," said John Andrew between his tears.[4]

It is obvious that Brenda is neglecting him, the child and their home. Tony is the only one not to see it. When the boy is accidentally killed things come to a head. Tony thinks only of Brenda, the blow she will have to suffer. He is unaware of his own mental state. If it was not for Mrs. Rattery, referred to by himself and Brenda as Jock Grant-Menzies's "Shameless Blonde," [5] who insists upon keeping him company while Jock tries to find Brenda in London, he might have gone out of his mind, under the impact of the shock. Superficial and vulgar as Mrs. Rattery seemed to the "noble" Lasts, she proves human and kind. She stays there as long as she is needed, then discreetly departs, almost unnoticed. Brenda appears shocked by the news only for a moment, when she thinks the "John" who is dead is Beaver and not her son; soon she is caught up again in the kind of life she has made her own. Her son, her husband, the "prison" of Hetton, all vanish in a mist of unreality. As excuses for her free life in London Brenda has used lies. In communicating with Tony she has resorted to lies all the time, lies so obvious as openly to invite the questions that

Tony would not ask. In a perverse way Brenda is straightforward. She does not try to appear other or better than she is. After her son's funeral she informs her husband, cynically yet without meaning to be cynical, that she will not return to Hetton, that their life together has lost its meaning and cannot continue.

Now the doubts Tony has always had about Brenda's life in London come to the surface. His sudden visit to her flat, the drunken bout with her former suitor Jock Grant-Menzies, his attempts at locating her, reflect a sort of inarticulate protest, long suppressed, against the way she has treated him. Yet after the final desertion, which is entirely incomprehensible to him, he still clings to his private vision of Brenda. He is ready to treat her generously in the divorce proceedings, to take all the blame on himself, and to give her a modest alimony, as much as he can without risking the loss of Hetton. Only Brenda's ultimate betrayal of his trust, and the fact that her attempt to get all she can out of him jeopardizes his proprietorship of Hetton, finally rouse his resentment. The Brenda who has neglected her husband and almost placidly accepted her boy's death, has not broken down his passive acceptance. Tony would have taken her back on equal terms, the minute she wanted him. But the Brenda who is ready to deprive him of Hetton is a traitor. She is no longer his Brenda. He can have no use for her.

For once Tony acts to protect his interests. Since he does not need a divorce he refuses to give her one. Hetton resumes its unique role in his life. Repairs are in progress. In the meantime why not go abroad? He has been outside England so little, once as a boy in France, once with his wife on their honeymoon. After he has decided to take a long trip abroad, he runs into Dr. Messinger and joins him in his expedition to Brazil. But on their advance through the jungle Dr. Messinger is killed in the rapids of the Amazon, and Tony is left alone, ravaged by malaria. Delirious, he relives the climactic events of his life. He talks to Brenda, goes through the agony of his boy's death. His own wasteful life is pitted against the waste of the overgrown jungle; the chaos of his ailing mind against the chaos of this unmapped world. He is found by Mr. Todd, a half-caste, who will keep him now, a prisoner for life, in order to have somebody to read Dickens aloud to him. The last chance of rejoining the civilized world, of returning to his own life, goes after three Englishmen in search of him are turned away by Mr. Todd while Tony is drugged into a profound sleep by the charmed herbs of the jungle. Not for anything would the provident Mr. Todd be deprived of the pleasure of reading, pleasures inaccessible to him, being illiterate, without his educated captive.

Tony is doomed to expiate the sins of his existence in the world by endlessly reading aloud to Mr. Todd. What are the sins, where has he gone astray, to have deserved such a lot? The fact that he made his wife take part in the family readings at Hetton, until she finally in an unguarded moment revealed her horror of it, is not enough to account for it. Why should Brenda be allowed to get away with her betrayal, to marry and "live happily ever after," while poor Tony is condemned to a lifelong penance serving a crazy man in a godforsaken jungle settlement?

Tony Last, whose very name seems to indicate that he is to terminate a long line of descent, comes from an ancient aristocratic family. His education, both at home and at school, proceeds strictly according to an old formula which was once meaningful but has outlived its usefulness. What at a much earlier date and under different circumstances would have made the scion of such a family an active member of the community to which he would have belonged, now contributes to the formation of a young man who only in appearance continues a living social tradition. Tony has not the least germ of public spirit. He is not really interested in any of his tenants' nor in his country's destiny, unless he is affected personally. He has no genuine attachments to people, either family or friends. The only attachment he feels is for Hetton, the family house, itself architecturally ruined —for it was deprived of aesthetic and historical value in the nineteenth century when, in the craze of the Gothic revival, some of the oldest buildings of the past were allowed to be ruined and deformed. Tony is impervious to aesthetic considerations, which have been left out of his ruling-class education. The only thing his social background and training have made him aware of is the importance of his ancestry, his social antecedents, and his own automatic importance as their successor. But the substance of this tradition has evaded him; only the mechanics, the form, remain. Tony himself has no personality, no individuality. Hetton represents his continuity in time. It alone lends him identity and enables him to exist.

Tony does not live like an individual being, expressing through his own life some amount, however modest, of individual enjoyment, some personal experience of living. The sole purpose his life has been given—an impoverishment of which he is obviously not aware—is to provide a link in the chain of family proprietorship. His love for Brenda runs on similar lines: she is an attractive woman who can provide an heir to Hetton. There is not much more in their relationship—on the surface so highly civilized, smooth, and decorous—than continuing the glories of the Lasts, sustaining the life at Hetton. Therefore Tony takes it for granted that Brenda should be as contented as he is to subject her desires, and sacrifice her evanescent youth and beauty, to the pattern of life at Hetton, and to accept the frugal life he offers her if it helps to keep the huge house, used in all its splendor only on one or two occasions each year and requiring a host of servants to keep up.

In the end Tony is punished for the greatest crime one can commit against life—for refusing to *be*. He is content to conform to outworn patterns of conduct without asking himself what they mean, or, if suspecting they have lost their meaning, without resenting their mean-inglessness. He goes to church regularly every Sunday and placidly listens to the sermons of a priest who re-peats texts he had written for overseas armies and talks of the jungle to uncomprehending English villagers. The incongruity bothers Tony as little as it does his tenants. His performance of his functions is automatic. So long as the moulds are preserved, the forms kept up, Tony feels safe and satisfied. The fact that the spirit that has cre-ated them and maintained them is gone never occurs to him. Tony's life, and the entire world he lives in, are really absurd, as deeply absurd as anything our post-1945 theater has imagined; yet Tony himself is not altogether diminished and static, and cannot quite be reduced to a figure illustrating a thesis.

Had nothing intervened, Tony would have happily continued his death-in-life. His wife, Brenda, would have indulged in one affair after the other, the one with John Beaver just happening to be the first. With a handy flat in London she could have led indefinitely her double life with a husband too much of a gentleman to inquire into her goings on, too little of a man to be able to react in any sense. Even John Andrew's death does not rouse Tony from his lethargic sleep into real life. It is Reggie's blackmail, endangering Hetton, that makes him act. For without Hetton his nonexistence can not continue. Het-ton, which conceals from him his own fear of life, alone can give his life the semblance of a meaning and so offer him protection.

While delirious in the jungle, his subconscious set free, Tony again invokes Brenda. His attachment to her, however mechanical and simple it has been, appears to have remained intact: even his subconscious will not register any change in their relationship.

> It was late in the afternoon when he first saw Brenda. For some time he he had been staring intently at the odd shape amidships . . . Then he saw that it was Brenda. "I'm sorry," he said. "I didn't see it was you. *You* wouldn't be frightened of a toy."

But she did not answer him. She sat as she used often to sit when she came back from London, huddled over her bowl of bread and milk . . .

"Just sit quiet here while I sling your hammock."

"Yes, I'll sit here with Brenda. I am so glad she could come. She must have caught the three-eighteen."

She was with him all that night and all the next day. He talked to her ceaselessly but her replies were rare and enigmatic. On the succeeding evening he had another fit of sweating. Dr. Messinger kept a large fire burning by the hammock and wrapped Tony in his own blanket. An hour before dawn Tony fell asleep and when he awoke Brenda had gone.[6]

At the end of his tether, tottering in fever through the jungle, the only thing that keeps Tony alive is his vision of Brenda.

"You're the first person who's spoken to me for days [Tony addresses Mr. Todd, who comes to rescue him]. The others won't stop. They keep bicycling by . . . I'm tired . . . Brenda was with me at first but she was frightened by a mechanical mouse, so she took the canoe and went off. She said she would come back that evening but she didn't. I expect she's staying with one of her new friends in Brazil . . . You haven't seen her have you?" [7]

In the depth of his being Tony has persisted in his repudiation of life. He has refused to experience life as it comes to him. He has refused to respond, to change with the changes imposed by the process of living. But life is not static, and no living being can oppose an immutable *state* to its permanent flow. If he tries, he not only fails; he will be punished. Life will take its revenge.

Tony has all the qualities of a well-trained English aristocrat. Shaken by fever, exposed to the hardships of the jungle in an almost hopeless situation, he behaves bravely; he stoically takes whatever comes along. He knows how to follow the pattern of gallant conduct, which always has a meaning when it is purposefully applied. Fortitude, courage, stoicism under adverse circumstances, the virtues of his class, have been bred into him. But here they no longer serve the serious purposes of life, only the risky, ill-prepared expedition of a fraud. Tony suffers the greatest of trials for no purpose whatever. This mockery of meaningful service, however, does not seem to bother him at all. Like a mechanical toy— like one of the mechanical mice that frighten the aborigines [8]—once wound up he goes through the motions, never wondering what their purpose is. Since Tony cannot direct his life and identify its progress toward some aim, there will be somebody who will know how to use him as a tool for his purposes. The first one to do so is the bogus explorer who needs another two hundred pounds for an expedition for which he probably, for good reasons, cannot get any funds, nor win the support of any scholarly society. When the dubious Dr. Messinger is killed, Mr. Todd, the half-caste, a still simpler and lower human being, turns up to use Tony as a means for his end, which is wholly mad. Tony, we have to say, seems to ask for it.

Descendent of a line of rulers, Tony Last is degraded from independence and authority, however faded, to a menial status. He becomes a sort of mechanical voice through which the contents of Dickens's novels can be communicated to the demented Mr. Todd. To prevent the reader and the author—and we note that even this, Waugh's most serious and humane novel, is presented as a ludicrous comedy—from falling into the pit of sentimentalism, life's little irony interferes at the end. For in a sense Tony is not so badly off. His new function in life has a certain appropriateness. He used to love reading aloud himself and mercilessly imposed his taste on others. Providence has seen to it that he shall have his fill.

Is Tony's fate tragic? It might have been if Tony had been capable of forming a "sense of it," to borrow Henry James's phrase. It is not in the tragic events themselves, James reminds us, it is in the sense of them as registered in our minds, that tragedy takes place. [9]

However one describes Tony's fate, it certainly ends in

complete degradation—of the man himself and of everything he stands for. Waugh drives home this implication
very artfully. The elite code of behavior remains intact.
Throughout the novel nobody ever raises his voice. In
awkward, sordid, preposterous situations the characters
could hardly be more polite to one another; they could
hardly show more surface consideration. Inside them,
and especially inside the central character, Tony Last,
there is such a vacuum that identity is lost.

Tony can exist and function only in reference to his
antecedents and his ancestral house. He himself, in his
own time and circumstance, has no meaning, no reality.
His death-in-life, expressed in his painful attempt to
preserve Hetton and thus force the past to continue into
the present, is ironically and wittily counterbalanced by
his return to life in the jungle. In England, in his own
ambience, he was dead inside, going automatically
through the inherited actions of life on the outside but
never enjoying them, never contributing any action of
his own to revivify the outworn moulds. In the jungle he
comes to life: officially reported as dead, he would break
out if he could and escape back into the life of men. But
he has missed his last chance.

6

Major Scobie

We are all of us resigned to death: it's life we aren't resigned to.[1]

Dissatisfied with the world he was born into, Graham Greene has embodied in his novels his search after a meaning in human life, a solution to the dilemma facing man in the modern world. The early novels reflecting his immediate reaction to contemporary developments seem, now that the author has reached his early sixties, a kind of exercise for the serious work that followed. In *Brighton Rock* [1938], *The Power and the Glory* [1940], *The Heart of the Matter* [1948], he expressed the idea that man's existence has a meaning only with reference to a transcendental deity. From a quest after God, who seems to elude one, in *Brighton Rock*, through a confrontation with him, to the latter's considerable disadvantage, in *The Power and the Glory*, Graham Greene came to treat God as the scapegoat in *The Heart of the Matter*, making him responsible for the injustice in this world.

Born in the early years of this century, and suffering in his boyhood the impact of World War I, Graham Greene found himself faced in his thirties with the inevitability of another even greater disaster. Human existence appeared to him as a man hunt. Whatever one did one could not avoid the fate of becoming either the hunted or the hunter. There seemed little to choose between the two alternatives, which were but the two sides of man's tragic, meaningless situation. After Pinkie, whose faith does not prevent him from being the leader of a gang of murderers, in *Brighton Rock*, Graham Greene created the Whiskey Priest, persecuted for his faith, in *The Power and Glory*. The priest is as unable to resist the urge to perform his office, to celebrate his God even if it involves the death of innocent people shot as hostages, as the police lieutenant is unable to hunt him. On both sides the logic of the situation is merciless. In the third novel of this [as it has been called] Catholic trilogy, Graham Greene comes to the most remorseless conclusion of all. In *The Heart of the Matter* the God he invokes is transformed into the arch-persecutor; it is he who has formed human existence on the pattern of the man hunt.

Negative, defeatist, destructive, whatever one may call such an attitude to reality, it confirmed Graham Greene in his conviction that mankind must have gone astray long ago. His curiosity as to where the wrong turning was taken could not, however, find assuagement. The deity he invoked had failed to offer a satisfactory answer. *The Heart of the Matter* contains the novelist's maturest statement of man's tragic situation, which deprives his life of value and himself of joy and makes him wish for death as the only solution, the best way out of an existence devoid of meaning.

In the work that followed, Greene took up the same theme on different levels, treating it now with the gravity of tragedy, now with the levity of light comedy. He tried his hand on the stage. None of this work, however, appears to have reached the seriousness of his approach to human destiny in *The Heart of the Matter*. No character he created, either before or after, expresses as forcefully as Major Scobie the author's conception of human personality, caught, as he saw it, between the hammer of sensibility and the anvil of physical desire: his refined awareness of himself, as the pinnacle of creation, helpless against the urges and lusts of the flesh, powerless to master the irrational. *The Heart of the Matter* brings to mind Conrad, one of the few novelists Graham Greene admires.

Major Scobie, Deputy Commissioner of Police, has been posted in a British colony in West Africa for fifteen years. When the time comes for the Commissioner to retire, Scobie, for reasons that are not divulged, is not appointed to succeed him. He takes this calmly as he would any sign of the malevolent world he lives in. He will neither "resign, retire, [nor] transfer." [2] He simply wants to stay in a place that he has come to like, in a queer, hardly comprehensible way. His wife, Louise, cannot take it the same way. She is a neurotic, selfish, vain woman who feels publicly disgraced and despises her husband for his acquiescence; she thinks she can no longer face anybody in the colony after her husband's failure to be promoted. She is an unlovable wife, but Scobie remains attached to her, though his love has long ago been transformed into pity, the more intense and uncontrollable since the loss of their daughter.

Driven by pity, he decides to borrow the money from the dangerous Syrian Yusef, the richest merchant in the place, to send his wife on a long journey to South Africa where, he thinks, he might ultimately join her. In any case he must grant her her wish. This is what he thinks he owes her: "No man could guarantee love for ever, but he had sworn fourteen years ago, at Ealing, silently, during the horrible little elegant ceremony among the lace and candles, that he would at least always see to it that she was happy." [3] And by this means Yusef has finally got hold of the rigid British Police Chief and will use him for his purposes.

So Scobie, "the Just," [4] known for his irreproachable conduct and simple honesty, is caught in the meshes of the crafty blackmailer. Soon after Louise's departure he gets involved in a love-affair with Helen, a young woman widowed in a shipwreck. Being a practising Catholic he cannot divorce his wife. Nor can he go against his pity for Helen, the poor child who "had never known her way around." [5] He cannot get an absolution for the sins in which he persists. Things take a nightmarish course and come to a head when his wife comes back before she is due. Scobie is blackmailed by Yusef into violating the law, set by his own country, to cover up the traces of his adultery. He is fully aware of the gravity of his action, but he is caught in a trap; his own recklessness has placed him at Yusef's mercy. Scobie falls deeper and deeper into corruption. To appease his wife he takes communion without repenting his sins. He knows he cannot deny his love to the helpless young woman, so he betrays his God. At this point his appointment to the post of Commissioner is announced. He cannot accept it now that he feels he is morally lost, sunk in sins beyond redemption. The only thing he thinks he can do is to writhdraw from this life in the least conspicuous way so as to inflict as little pain on others as possible. Suicide is the way out, but for a Catholic this must mean eternal damnation. Scobie's pity for others, however, seems to bar him from pity for himself: "human love . . . had robbed him of love for eternity." [6] He carefully plans and executes his suicide so that it looks like death by heart failure.

We first see Scobie through the eyes of Harris, a British official, who distrusts him, and of Wilson, newly arrived from London to spy on them all and on Scobie in particular, as it seems:

> "Look down there," Harris said, "look at Scobie."
> A vulture flapped and shifted on the iron roof and Wilson looked at Scobie. He looked without interest in obedience to a stranger's direction, and it seemed to him that no particular interest attached to the squat grey-haired man walking alone up Bond Street.
> "He loves 'em much," Harris said, "he sleeps with 'em."
> "Is that the police uniform?"
> "It is. Our great police force. A lost thing . . ."
> [Wilson's] eyes followed Scobie up the sun-drowned street. Scobie stopped and had a word with a black man in a white panama: a black policeman passed by, saluting smartly. Scobie went on.

"Probably in the pay of the Syrians too, if the truth were known."

"The Syrians?"

"This is the original Tower of Babel," Harris said. "West Indians, Africans, real Indians, Syrians, Englishmen, Scotsmen in the Office of Works. Irish priests, French priests, Alsatian priests."

"What do the Syrians do?"

"Make money. They run all the stores up-country and most of the stores here. Run diamonds too."

"Hasn't he got a wife here?"

"Who? Oh, Scobie. Rather. He's got a wife. Perhaps if I had a wife like that, I'd sleep with niggers too. You'll meet her soon. She's the city's intellectual. She likes art, poetry . . . Poor old Scobie." [7]

How far does this impression of Scobie coincide with reality? Scobie is a just man. His honesty in dealing with the "niggers" [8] and trying to make justice work has probably earned him many enemies. He is humane towards the local people, and this has contributed to the gossip about his sleeping with local women and even being in the pay of the Syrians. At first indignant against the "black skin" [9] for their expert ability to circumvent the law, he has gone beyond hatred—"during his fifteen years [he has] passed through the dangerous stages: now lost in the tangle of lies he felt an extraordinary affection for these people who paralyzed an alien form of justice by so simple a method." [10] Harris himself probably does not believe what he says about Scobie. He just vents his hostility for a man who is withdrawn and correct in his bearing, whose reserve—he keeps them all at a distance —has been mistaken for arrogance. How can others understand what has attached Scobie to the place when he himself can hardly account for it.

Why, he wondered, swerving the car to avoid a dead pye-dog, do I love this place so much? Is it because here human nature hasn't had time to disguise itself? Nobody here could ever talk ubout a heaven on earth. Heaven remained rigidly in its proper place on the other side of

death, and on this side flourished the injustices, the cruel-
ties, the meanness, that elsewhere people so cleverly
hushed up. Here you could love human beings nearly as
God loved them, knowing the worst: you didn't love a
pose, a pretty dress, a sentiment artfully assumed.[11]

Scobie's tragic destiny—or is it only pathetic?—comes
from his attitude to people and things. He has seen the
seamy side from too close; permanently confronted with
it, he has lost faith in man. His joy of life is gone forever.
He is happiest when he is alone, in peace, with nobody
having any claim on him or rousing his feelings. He does
not trust sentiment, for it corrupts worse than money.
And this is the case with him: "he had been corrupted
by sentiment. Sentiment was the more dangerous, because you couldn't name its price." [12] Since he cannot
control his compassion, his pity, he is safe only in solitude. Such are the moments he treasures and remem-
bers: "Except for the sound of the rain, on the road, on
the roofs, on the umbrella, there was absolute silence:
only the dying moan of the sirens continued for a moment or two to vibrate within the ear. It seemed to
Scobie later that this was the ultimate border he had
reached in happiness: being in darkness, alone, with rain
falling, without love or pity." [13]

All we know about Scobie's past is that he married
fourteen years ago and that he is a convert to Catholicism. We are not told what led him to this step, but we
learn by implication that he needed something beyond
this "world so full of misery," [14] something that would
make life worthwhile and lend importance to his sense
of himself, give a meaning to his existence. When he
prayed before sleep he used to add an Act of Contrition.
It was a formality to him,

> not because he felt himself free from serious sin but
> because it had never occurred to him that his life was
> important enough one way or another. He didn't drink, he
> didn't fornicate, he didn't even lie, but he never regarded
> this absence of sin as virtue. When he thought about it at
> all, he regarded himself as a man in the ranks, the mem-

ber of an awkward squad, who had no opportunity to
break the more serious military rules.[15]

When he married Louise and promised her life-long
love, he really meant it. Ever since, he has felt responsible for her: "When he was young, he had thought love
had something to do with understanding, but with age
he knew that no human being understood another. Love
was the wish to understand, and presently with constant
failure the wish died, and love died too perhaps or
changed into painful affection, loyalty, pity." [16] Now
that he has to break the news of his failure to her, he
feels guilty. He would do anything to avoid giving pain
to another. He started out with hope. He believed what
he promised her, but he has been overwhelmed by what
he saw. Life in all its nakedness, undisguised as it was in
civilized Europe, has proved too much for him. Here he
felt he must keep himself in hand, control his emotions:
"This isn't a climate for emotion. It's a climate for
meanness, malice, snobbery, but anything like hate or
love drives a man off his head." [17] His wife soon lost her
charm for him. The child that gave meaning to their life
together died. Some people, we know, can stand more
adversity than others. Any pressure one can stand is good
for one. But one can never know when one is going to
break. And Scobie has broken under the pressure he was
exposed to.

The fact that he was not promoted when he should
have been gave him the last push. He felt he had somehow failed his wife, had not lived up to the vows he had
taken before the altar. He himself is not bothered at
being a failure. He would have been far more surprised
to be a success, for he cannot believe that a decent man
can ever find happiness. "Point me out the happy man
and I will point you out either egotism, selfishness, evil
—or else an absolute ignorance." [18] Success is "of the
Devil's party." [19] Against his wife's reproaches, against
the cruelty and the meanness of the world, he takes
refuge in his pity. This is the only way he can retain a
modicum of self-respect. If your love for others gets

transformed into profound loyalty, or pity for the help-less, then it may still have some meaning. You are ele-vated into being a sort of guardian of the weak and the unprotected. Scobie's sense of responsibility, required by his functions as a policeman, grows out of all proportion. He feels guilty for Louise's misery, for her aging face, for her lack of charm, for the fact that she had come to him young and was now growing old. He will go any length to atone for his wife's unhappiness. He forgets that "no human being can really understand another and no one can arrange another's happiness." [20] He is ready to break the law, the professional code of ethics, to alleviate her pains. His disintegration begins. His power of dealing out justice weakens: he cannot prosecute the Captain of the *Esperanza* for his illicit letter, since he himself is going to take a loan from Yusef, although he knows that a police official should never become beholden to a dis-honest merchant on whose dark dealings he should keep an eye.

Scobie has never been able to stand the sight of human suffering, especially that of children. He has tried to avoid the agony of his own daughter's dying. But destiny makes him witness the agony of another child dying in a hospital after having been rescued from a shipwreck. "To be a human being one had to drink the cup." [21] From the outset Scobie has had anticipations of what will befall him. He sees his suicide in that of young Pemberton, which he has to investigate; he anticipates his criminal bond with Yusef much before he has him-self become prey to blackmail. His forebodings give his life the nightmarish coloring of something that has been preordained and could not be avoided. In this respect they are saturated with the atmosphere of a neurotic age, the years of the war—the action takes place during the war—and the years immediately preceding the war when mankind stood watching its approaching doom doing nothing to prevent it, as though sunk into a profound sleep and helplessly dreaming into existence some irre-versible catastrophe.

It is his compulsive pity that drives Scobie into his affair with Helen, who has been widowed only three weeks after her marriage and made to endure an eternity of forty days in a lifeboat. He will always remember his first vision of Helen, who "must have been still at school" when "this damned war started," "carried into his life on a stretcher, grasping a stamp-album, with her eyes fast shut." [22] This is more than enough to attach Scobie's devotion. He still can help, take on the responsibility for others: "It was the stamp-album and not the face that haunted his memory, for no reason that he could understand, and the wedding-ring loose on the finger, as though a child had dressed up." [23] He is painfully susceptible to details that seem to reveal the essence of things and he responds most acutely to the pathos of it.

Looking after the young widow, as he first proposes to do, is something that seems to rejuvenate him, giving him a new lease on life. But he is a man and hardly fifty, and he cannot resist lust. His selfless love of the destitute woman turns into a passionate love-affair. Once he has broken away from his moral code, there is nothing to stop him. The sad, defeatist philosophy that makes him look upon life as a kind of trial by a severe judge, a Jehovah in the garb of Christ, cannot make him fight for his own security, his own happiness. Life seems to him "immeasurably long." "Couldn't the test of man have been carried out in fewer years? Couldn't we have committed our first major sin at seven, have ruined ourselves for love or hate at ten, have clutched at redemption on a fifteen-year-old death bed?" [24] The more Scobie falls into corruption, the less he tries to resist it.

Scenes of jealousy, like those he had with Louise, soon develop. No woman wants only pity. Helen does not want compassion, saintly sacrifice. She wants a love that is not shared with another. But as a Catholic Scobie cannot divorce. He cannot bring himself to separate from his wife, because he would not hurt her. He can only sacrifice himself, the "unpitiable." [25] To assuage

Helen's jealousy, her resentment of his cautiousness, he writes the fatal letter that gets into Yusef's hands. Scobie is aware of the risk, he knows that it may be his undoing, but he cannot resist the impulse. Yet even the inexperienced child-woman Helen begins to feel, what Louise must have felt before her, that somehow Scobie is failing her "in manhood." [26] This seems to be the source of all the tragedy, and this is what the perceptive Scobie, who looks into his mind more than is good for him, will never face. He senses it indistinctly—"It seemed to him that he must have failed in some way in manhood" [27]—but he never stops to consider what this means. He would rather accept his own damnation than face this fact. The inner conflict mounts. He is divided against himself. To win absolution he must break with Helen. Her courage —she insists they should break—and her "heart-breaking tenderness" [28] produce the opposite effect; they only bind him the stronger to her.

Persecuted by a sense of guilt towards Louise, with Wilson and the others spying on him and closing in on his dealings with Yusef, Scobie is ultimately exposed to the last and the worst of persecutions. His quarrel with God begins. He cannot fail Louise, so he cannot desert her; he cannot fail Helen, so he must continue in adultery; he cannot resist Yusef, for exposure of his letter would have hurt his wife. He cannot avoid sinning against God's commandments, so he is barred from confession and communion. But Louise would have him commit this the greatest of sins for a practising Catholic. On her insistence, and to alleviate her suspicions, he takes communion, though full of sin. He betrays his God and accepts his damnation. Like a criminal magnetically lured towards his own disaster, while seeking to avoid hurt, Scobie hurts the more. With the loss of integrity goes the loss of trust. His devoted boy, Ali, who has served him for fifteen years, is the first victim. Sins seem to pile on his head. He feels that his life cannot go on in this way, and yet it never occurs to him that he should face the situation and take an action.

Scobie lacks simple courage. He hides behind pity for others. Like Conrad's Jim before him, he cannot realize that the refusal to witness other people's suffering is cowardice in disguise. Jim could not face the spectacle of eight hundred people fighting for seven boats; Scobie cannot face the suffering of Louise, the woman who has failed him as much as he has failed her, whose failure is as great as his own. He is magnetized by failure—but does not understand his own condition. He has his doubts about succeeding, and yet how profound is his vanity. When his promotion to the post of Commissioner is announced, Scobie thinks: "all this need not have happened. If Louise had stayed I should never have loved Helen: I would never have been blackmailed by Yusef, never have committed that act of despair. I would have been myself still—the same self . . . not this broken cast." [29] He will not face his own weakness, his lack of manhood: "But, of course, he told himself, it's only because I have done these things that success comes. I am of the Devil's party. He looks after his own in this world. I shall go now from damned success to damned success, he thought with disgust." [30]

Scobie, the "Just," who thinks he must carry the responsibility not only for his functions as a policeman but for the happiness of all those whom chance throws in his way, lacks courage to take the responsibility for himself. He shifts it elsewhere, now to God, now to the Devil. Consciousness of his own lack of fortitude, however disguised by an exaggerated sense of responsibility, is as unacceptable to him as it was to Conrad's Jim. He reacts to it in his own utterly negative way. Jim at least confirmed human values at the cost of his life. Scobie denies human values and turns to a transcendental God-figure instead. He hides behind the figure of the Christian God for a long time, but God cannot help him, for He also demands fortitude, self-discipline, courage in adversity. He demands the confirmation of life, He cannot condone the escape from it, in suicide.

Like a degraded Hamlet, Scobie cannot act openly

and directly, even within his mind. He deludes himself into believing that he is doing all this for his love of man and that God, who likewise loves man, will therefore have consideration for him at the last judgment. And all the time he knows that this is not the right interpretation. He begins to attribute to God his own deficiencies. God becomes his scapegoat. He piles on God his weakness, his sham pity, his failure. Since he is doing what Christ has done, why should God not accept the sacrifice of his life for "human love"? [31] Scobie's vanity mounts: he acts as if he is himself "the beginning and the end." [32] Through his lack of courage he suffers to the point of losing judgment: he equates hysteria with honesty,[33] madness with honesty.[34] He takes human justice, the law, into his hands and breaks it for his own purposes; he takes upon himself the justice of the Christian God, and sins against His commandments. He tries to be more than man and becomes less.[35] On the surface the humblest of men, he loses all humility. He proclaims the right to decide for himself on matters beyond his control and demands to be accepted at his own valuation. And if as the book's motto seems to say, Scobie is to be taken as a kind of modern saint,[36] he is a saint who gives glamor to failure, glories in the degradation of man, and ultimately in the annihilation of human life.

Major Scobie embodies the world's rush into disaster in the late thirties. He cannot accept the destructiveness of the world he lives in yet feels helpless to resist it. Like a corruption it begins to infect him as well and his picture of life. Human existence is a man-hunt, in which you are either the hunted or the hunter. You are trapped into marriage, into pity, into a love affair—the result is always the same. In this corrupt world your good intentions turn against you. Attempting to help those you think are dependent on you, those for whose misery you feel responsible, you are trapped into a kind of partnership in crime. You are trapped with those who spy on you; you are trapped with your God, who keeps your conscience alive to your misdeeds.

But all this is not really a true account of human existence, nor is it borne out by the particulars of the novel. Scobie is hunted throughout by his own unacknowledged weakness. Born into a complicated world over which darkness is rapidly spreading, endowed with acute perceptiveness, full of insight into other men, susceptible to the prevailing atmosphere, quickly responsive to people and things, and fundamentally kind, he has no courage to cast his potentialities off, as Conrad would have put it. With a romantically surcharged sensibility he lacks the daring that would "alter the whole conception of what is possible" [37] and give him the self-esteem that would keep him above board. He does not love life, he does not love himself, and so he cannot love anybody else. He does have, fitfully, the courage to look into his own sins, but he has not the courage for the ultimate confrontation with his own weakness. He must lull himself with a belief in his pity for others, his responsibility for other people's happiness. All the time, at the back of his mind, the consciousness that all this is fake is latent and alive. This consciousness he persistently ignores. Since he cannot be a man, he tries to be a saint. He will be even more than that. He will go beyond what Christ has done. Christ gave his life for eternal bliss. Scobie will sacrifice his love of eternity to his love of men. He will jeopardize his eternal bliss and accept damnation, together with death, for the sake of the happiness of others, or rather to spare the others undue suffering in this world of misery. Scobie's masochistic drive towards self-torture and finally death is disguised by his belief that he is sacrificing himself for others.

This is yet another, a fourth variation of that nihilism in the modern conception of life that our inquiry keeps uncovering. The wish for death popped its ugly head out for a brief moment at the opening of this century, in Conrad's *Lord Jim*, where, unable to accept the violation of his illusion about life, and about himself, incapable of acknowledging his own weakness, the hero can only die. So, too, in *Mrs. Dalloway*, fear of life and the refusal to participate in it lead to death. Tony Last, for his part, has lost his hold on life very young, in the very circumstance of his growing up. He only realizes the fact that he is alive when confronted with a protracted death-in-life in the heart of the Brazilian jungle. But he cannot die, for he has never lived. Unlike the above characters Major Scobie is given an acute sense of life. He participates in it so intensely that he can see through its shams and disguises. This is why the nakedness of life in an African colony appeals to him more than its civilized counterpart in Europe. His vanity is apparent, yet he does not suffer from overmuch self-love. He has gone to the other extreme. Having lost the joy of life, he denies love to himself. He comes to despise himself to the point of an irreversible loathing. He cannot any longer carry the burden of himself.

From Jim to Scobie, we seem to have come full circle: from the readiness to die [if not positively to live] for the dignity of man and of oneself as human being to a determination to disappear from life as obscurely as one has tried to live, in a world of misery where one can only meet degradation. Jim dies "under a cloud." [38] But his death is deplored by those he protected. He is condemned by the woman he loved, but she will never forget him. He is loved by his friends. Both his weakness and his final self-forgetful fortitude make him a representative of mankind with all the dignity of a Hamlet. Scobie reduces human existence to the depth not only of misery but of abasement. He glories in defeat, deifies failure. All human values are desecrated. He even drags God down to be desecrated as well. The courage and hope that Conrad discovers in Jim's story, and the standard of fortitude Jim is held up to, are characteristic of those closing years of the nineteenth century when the neurosis that springs from a dwindling confidence in the stability of the human individual had only begun surreptitiously to undermine the belief in man. At the time Graham Greene was creating his Scobie this process had reached its climax. The worst fears inspired by the contemplation of man's conduct were confirmed by the nightmarish horrors of reality. Unable to find in himself the source of strength to resist, Scobie completely collapsed under the pressure of the tragic actuality. His failure is the failure of the will to live, and it is absolute.

7

Mrs. Jardine

> Sometimes . . . the source is vitiated, choked. Then people
> live frail, wavering lives, their roots cut off from what should
> nourish them. That is what happens to people when love is
> betrayed—murdered.[1]

By placing his characters into situations which may appear unnatural, verging on the melodramatic, the novelist can make them reveal themselves and yield a new insight into human beings. However grim the reality disclosed in such treatment it may be rendered with such force that the poetic, timeless truth that emerges cannot be denied. Rosamond Lehmann, in her novels, is above all interested in people, in their inner lives. Emotional crises, caused by adverse circumstances, that bring them into conflict with themselves and with other people usually less sensitive than themselves, form the core of most of her writing, which is centred on women in the full process of their development from childhood into adolescence, womanhood, and old age. It is the grace, the delicacy of perception, the psychological insight, and the artistic rendering of intimate experience that have attracted readers to her work. She would, however, hardly be noted as more than a graceful minor literary artist had she not created the figure of Mrs. Jardine in *The Ballad and the Source* [1944], a book that both confirms the validity of her own conception of the novel and raises her into the ranks of those modern novelists who have explored the hitherto unknown, or rather unavowed, abysses of the human psyche.

According to Rosamond Lehmann "There is a 'still centre' for the novelist as for any other artist." In this respect the novel is not different from the poem: "Its

97

genesis is the image, or isolated images which have become embedded in the mass of accumulated material in the author's 'centre.' " Rosamond Lehmann sets herself to write when she can no longer resist the insistent pressure of these images to emerge from her creative consciousness. As though the isolated images that have become created in her "centre" have suddenly been released, in *The Ballad and the Source* they take the lead and guide the pen of the mesmerized author, who reveals more about human nature than she herself would have been ready to admit under conscious control.

The delusion embodied in Mrs. Jardine that the role we act in life has just as much reality as our real being, i.e., that the attempt to present ourselves in a different, elevated form is on the whole praiseworthy, motivated as it is by an ideal of human conduct, and that it does neither ourselves nor anybody else any harm, would not in itself have assured this character the important place given her in this essay. Neither would it have contributed to Rosamond Lehmann's well-deserved reputation as a writer with an exceptional insight into the human mind's inner disturbances, had she not managed to present in Sibyl Jardine an arche-type of a central human experience, that of the woman—a mother in this instance—who has not been cast for the part she is required to play.

Sibyl Jardine is the source. It is through her that the "fount of life" should rise and flow to be passed on to the new generations. As mother she should partake in the cycle of creation and assist life in its victorious march forward. But since her being has been poisoned the limpid fount of life that runs through her is vitiated. The waters that spring from the source are grim and troubled. They cannot nourish new life and give it the vitality it needs to survive unscathed the pains of growth to which every living being is exposed. Deprived of the revitalizing protection of motherhood life rushes towards a destructive tragic end. The source is no longer the spring of life triumphant. As in a tragic ballad it is death that triumphs; its victims are scattered all over the field.

Mrs. Jardine's is a complicated story of a talented, even brilliant woman whose assumption of motherhood poisons her being. It gives her own life an uneven twisted course, and brings disaster not only upon her own daughter but also her daughter's children. This is the impression one gains on first reading the intriguing novel, *The Ballad and the Source*. On rereading it, however, we find that Mrs. Jardine, like persons in life, seems to require more than one interpretation. The frustrating burden of motherhood is just one clue, the first, into the complicated labyrinth of Mrs. Jardine's being. For it is in her whole being, that we have to look for a satisfying explanation of this character, whose searching analytical mind makes her as representative of our times as any character in the modern English novel, although the author has placed her in the England of her own childhood, between 1910 and the early years of World War I, 1916.

What makes Mrs. Jardine a most vivid character and lends her the verisimilitude of a truly significant character in fiction is the way we get to know her. We are not brought face to face with her, nor do we get introduced to her by the omniscient author. A letter comes from her. Letters give personal coloring—since Richardson they have functioned also as confessions—especially if the person who has written them is as passionate a letter-writer as Mrs. Jardine. The comments that accompany the reading of it throw light simultaneously from different angles. The character takes on the complexity of a person existing in real life and rouses a corresponding interest, at once superficial, out of sheer curiosity, and deeply inward.

Mrs. Jardine make her impression first upon the imagination of the ten-year-old Rebecca. Rebecca is the chief narrator, the focus of our attention, but—in the manner of Henry James's *What Maisie Knew*—she is not herself the source of information. Rebecca does not know a thing. She has no experience or knowledge of life, of people or things, beyond what her age and her sheltered life would have brought to her attention. She is the innocent eye in which the varying information she eagerly tries to collect to satisfy her almost uncanny though benevolent curiosity are for the very reason of her innocence reflected without distortion. Placed by chance in direct and close relation to the chief actors in the drama and in particular to Mrs. Jardine, Rebecca consistently and unobtrusively plays her role. Her innocence guarding her from corrosion, she does not get infected with the corruption she is brought so close to. She successfully acts her role of intermediary to the very end. She comes out intact, with her integrity inviolate, the richer and probably the less liable to corruption for this early initiation into the equivocality of human appearance, the disparity between the roles people assume and the being laboring underneath.

Mrs. Jardine imposes herself on Rebecca's childhood world. She insists upon reestablishing a contact that has been broken long ago. Rebecca's father is on guard. He does not welcome the reappearance of his mother's former friend, associated as she seems to have been with nothing but trouble and finally insult. His comment, "She'd charm the birds off the trees," [2] together with her own mother's reluctant, half-hearted acceptance of Mrs. Jardine's invitation, symptoms revealing enough to an adult mind, seem to whet Rebecca's appetite for more. She is immediately taken in by Mrs. Jardine's appearance:

> She gave the impression of arms outstretched, so welcomingly did she surge forward to meet us. She was dressed in a long gown of pale blue with wide sleeves embroidered thickly with blue, rose and violet flowers. She had a white fleecy wrap round her shoulders, and on her head, with its pile of fringed, puffed, curled white hair, a large Panama hat trimmed with a blue liberty scarf artistically knotted, the ends hanging down behind. She was small and rather stocky, with short legs and little feet shod in low-heeled black slippers with tongues and paste buckles . . . Her lips and cheeks were dry, warm, the skin so crinkled all over

with faint lines it seemed a fine-meshed net. The most noticeable things about her were the whiteness of her face, the paleness of her large eyes, and the strong fullness and width of her mouth. Her teeth were regular, splendid, untouched by age.[3]

Mrs. Jardine's outspokenness, her free expression of feelings worded in an artistic literary style, her whole pose, the act she puts on, impress the romantically susceptible Rebecca and deprive her of a critical sense. Rebecca's infatuation attracts the attention of the vain old woman. She makes Rebecca from the outset a kind of confidante. Entranced by this unusual apparition from the world of the adult, Rebecca begins to look around for clues. In a typically childish way she persists in tireless search. Overheard and half-finished sentences pointing to something less than favorable make her the more eager to find her own explanation, though one that will not diminish Mrs. Jardine in her eyes. Chance remarks like that of her father's, her mother's obvious reserve, Mrs. Jardine's granddaughter's hostility, almost hatred—though Maisie has become her closest friend— cannot be reconciled with the Mrs. Jardine whose charm has won Rebecca completely over.

Put on the scent by Maisie's mention of Tilly, her grandmother's former maid and now a seamstress who comes to their home twice a year to do some sewing, Rebecca tries to get out of this vivid cockney as much as she can. From Tilly Rebecca learns about the ardent friendship between her own grandmother, already advanced in years, and the seductive young girl, Miss Sibyl. With undiminished admiration for the irresistible charm of the then beautiful Miss Sibyl, Tilly revives the past and brings Mrs. Jardine's story close to the present. Mrs. Jardine herself gives Rebecca her own version and covers the part deliberately left out by Tilly. Finally Maisie fills in the remaining part by taking the story up where Mrs. Jardine has left off and bringing it to the present moment. This information, together with the family's direct relations with Mrs. Jardine, the letters she writes to

Rebecca's mother from France, ultimately creates a complete figure. The portrait gains in depth through its multiplicity of facets, each from another source. The attempt of extremely different people, who have met her or shared her life at various times and under various circumstances, to elucidate the character from their own peculiar angles and make their own valuation, bring Mrs. Jardine even closer to life. All this sifted through the mind of a girl who from a child of ten grows in the course of this exploration into her fourteenth and fifteenth year, brings into being a fully dimensional character with the completeness and intense complexity of a figure in life.

Events take an adverse course in Sibyl's life when she decides to join her lover and leave her husband, Mr. Herbert, to whom she has been married for a few years. She believes that she will be able to get her little daughter, Ianthe; she cannot give her up to her father. Her tireless efforts culminate in a fruitless attempt to steal the child, which makes Mr. Herbert give up diplomatic service, remove to an estate in Kent, bar the windows against her and put Ianthe under strong guard. The girl is educated not in ignorance of her mother but in hatred of her. Sibyl spends years of her life in penury. All the time she keeps an eye on her daughter. Ianthe's visits with Rebecca's grandmother in London, where she is taken care of by Tilly, seem to offer her a chance to get in touch with her child. It is the former's refusal to assist in this, since it is contrary to Mr. Herbert's express desire, that sets Sibyl against her old friend and breaks the friendship Mrs. Jardine is at such pains to renew in her old age.

The next chance to get hold of Ianthe comes after Mr. Herbert's death at a time Sibyl, married for the second time to Colonel Jardine, is again established in fortune and society. Sibyl, as she professes, has lived for this moment, but her daughter again escapes her. Provisions made in her father's will have secured Ianthe against her mother. She herself is closed to her mother. As a result of her lonely life and peculiar, unwholesome education, Ianthe is withdrawn into herself. High-strung and passionate by nature, she ardently desires communion with others, yet she cannot open up and establish a sound contact with people and the world round her. Finally, when Ianthe's own children become practically orphaned, being deserted by their mother with their father dying of cancer, they come to Sibyl. Now their sole guardian, Sibyl at last has her wish. Instead of Ianthe, who has repudiated her, she has three helpless children looking up to her to mould their destiny. It is at this moment of triumph that she tries to reestablish the broken link with the descendants of the only person she seems ever to have loved, Rebecca's grandmother.

Mrs. Jardine knows exactly what the children need. She has all the fortune of Colonel Jardine to work with and it does not seem to be negligible. She sets about her task with youthful zest and energy, in spite of age and declining health. Nobody seems to know about Ianthe's goings on. What the reader can glean from Mrs. Jardine's own confessions is that Ianthe has grown into a mentally perturbed woman, with no physical hold on life. She is, as Mrs. Jardine puts it, a "mirror haunter," a term she explains to the astounded Rebecca as follows: "She had built herself a room of mirrors. She never looked out straight into the light, at objects, at other people's faces. She looked into these mirrors and saw the whole of creation as images of herself thrown back at her. On them she brooded, adoring, fearing what she saw." And the reason why she has done it, according to Mrs. Jardine, is her fear of the world.

> When people are afraid they dare not look outward for fear of getting too much hurt. They shut themselves up and look only at pictures of themselves, because these they can adapt and manipulate to their needs without interference, or wounding shocks. The world sets snares for their self-love. It betrays them. So they look in the mirrors and see only what flatters and reasures them; and so they imagine they are not betrayed.[4]

Ianthe could not sublimate her being in her love for her husband, or her children. Erotic in temperament but suffering from the suppression of normal instincts by the circumstances of her education, she could not settle down for long to any intellectual effort. She became a spiritual vagrant, bound to meet a tragic end. Mrs. Jardine's explanation of the cause that accounts for both her daughter's mental instability and her beloved youngest granddaughter Cherry's wavering health points to the truth: "Her vitality has suffered some natal or pre-natal injury. The source rises in her—then flags and wavers down again. It is not stable. That is *her* inheritance." She explains to the bewildered Rebecca:

> "The source, Rebecca! The fount of life—the source, the quick spring that rises in illimitable depths of darkness and flows through every living thing from generation to generation. It is what we feel mounting in us when we say: 'I know! I love! I *am!*'
> "Sometimes . . . the source is vitiated, choked. Then people live frail, wavering lives, their roots cut off from what should nourish them. That is what happens to people when love is betrayed—murdered." [5]

This, like all of Mrs. Jardine's investigations into herself, though true, is shaped so as to give the kind of answer she herself can accept, an explanation that will allow no suspicion as to her own responsibility. It is meant to seem wholly plausible to Rebecca. And yet throughout, as once for a twinkling of a moment in Tilly's attic,[6] or once in the beautiful garden where Mrs. Jardine tells Rebecca her story, the susceptible child feels the presence of evil incarnate in the beautiful envelope of the charmer. "For the first time in her actual presence the sense pierced me directly: that she was wicked. A split second's surmise. But when the next moment I looked up at her, there was her profile lifted beautifully above me, serene and reassuring as a symbol in stone." [7] The very way in which Mrs. Jardine clinically dissects the pathetic figure of her own daughter, without a trace of motherly love but only a kind of enjoyment of motherhood as power, undermines Rebecca's faith. The accumulation of a great many intimations of this kind, in Mrs. Jardine's own words and in the words and actions of others, overcomes her. For a moment she fears madness: "I writhed in my chair, pierced by a chilling thought. Could Mrs. Jardine be—not quite right in the head? . . . And I alone with her?" [8]

Her brief but potent moment of insecurity in the presence of this "unearthy" person prepares both Rebecca and the reader for the final revelation of Mrs. Jardine's essential being. Consistently advancing on her course through life, frustrated in her desires and infatuations, loathed by Ianthe, unable to admit the facts of suffering or sickness [as with her grandchild, Cherry] among those near to her, for whom she may be responsible, she passes finally from being hated to being profoundly pitied. Even Maisie, who holds her responsible for Cherry's death, can see her as embodying the tragedy of a passionate nature thwarted in her ambitions, made sterile in spite of her talent for life and her refined apprehension of the most abstract beauty; a woman who had everything she needed to make life equal to art, brave enough never to accept defeat and yet meeting nothing but defeat.

In the end Mrs. Jardine is left all alone: her only daughter in a lunatic asylum, her grandson killed in World War I, her beloved granddaughter Cherry buried. Her husband, whom she has made into a slave in his life-time, having curtailed her in his will, she is reduced even in her fortune. The only result of her painstaking efforts to make her life rich, to give and create, seems to be Maisie, the stocky, matter-of-fact girl without charm and determined not to get married, since attachment, as it seems to her, can only bring harm and continue the lineage of torment and victimization in her family. "I intend to have it written on my tombstone: Here lies a person who never needed anybody, so she never did anybody *any harm*." [9] Mrs. Jardine could tolerate Maisie, but she could not love her, since she could never have any power over her. The source is to be choked altogether. It must dry out to prevent more pain and suffering. Mrs. Jardine's life seems to have served no other purpose but to transform the source of life into the source of death. Her ceaseless efforts to bring beauty into her own life and that of others have brought nothing but the tragic misery of hatred, madness, and sterility.

Is Mrs. Jardine what she normally appears to little Rebecca, or is she what even the young girl at times dimly feels, the dark witchlike figure enveloped in the beautiful scarves, endowed with unparalleled beauty and charm the better to fulfill her mission of dark revenge? Rebecca could not get rid of a "vision of her, high on the watch tower of a castle in France, directing upon us searchlight eyes over wastes of winter dark and ocean. Her glittering face blazed in the firmament, savage, distraught, unearthly: Enchantress Queen in an antique ballad of revenge." [10] Snow White's stepmother comes to mind— but then do not all such stories reflect the motifs of human conduct much more closely than one is ready to admit, prone as one is to deceive oneself about human nature? What brings the fairy-tale stepmother to mind is the metaphor of *mirrors*. Her chief concern is that she should be the most beautiful woman in the world. And she must never have children to compete with. This is where the core of the problem seems to reside; it is here that we should look for the final clue to Mrs. Jardine's character.

Oddly enough, she has something essential in common with so different a character as Clarissa Dalloway. Like Clarissa, Sibyl Jardine uncannily sees into herself. What she finds in herself, she projects on others, or she erects a general truth about life, about human depravity, unaware that she is speaking for herself and that what she says is actually most directly applicable to herself. Mrs. Jardine is the one to bring in the term "mirror-haunter" [11] in talking about her daughter. How far this is applicable to the latter, the reader is not in a position to decide. Ianthe remains vague throughout. Even if she does correspond to her mother's decription, she does so by direct inheritance. If Ianthe has "built herself a room of mirrors," [12] Mrs. Jardine has reduced the whole world to a "room of mirrors." Unlike Ianthe she is involved in life, but in her own way. She plunges into it, but she can never give herself to it.

This is what she has in common with Clarissa. For reasons as different as the two women, she cannot give herself to her love for her first husband. Whatever the value of Tilly's cockney comment—" 'e was better furnished in the top storey than 'e was elsewhere, was that joker" [13]—Sibyl never loved him. She was attracted by the kind of love he could offer her, highly cultivated and rich as he was and posted in Paris in diplomatic service. She could not be sublimated in her love for her daughter either. The more she spoke, or rather wrote, about her Ianthe, about her special grace, her beauty, and the future they were going to give her, the less Tilly and her mistress trusted her. All this was partly the result of her exalted conception of what the rich life of a beautiful woman should be, partly of an unconscious attempt to cover up her own growing restlessness, which she discovered in herself as soon as the possibilities of acting the hostess of a diplomat, meeting admiring eyes, and having a daughter, were exhausted. Her love-affair did not last long. She was alone again, devoured by her longing for her child.

One thing mirror-haunters cannot accept is defeat. The only reality is their glittering reflection in the eyes of others. They are, with all the bravery and even gallantry with which they act, timid, afraid of life. They are not daring enough to plunge into the world, but only into their fantasy of it. They are not ready to take on the consequences, the responsibility, for they cannot size themselves up or acknowledge the internal flaw that holds them back.

If their attitude to life is like that of Clarissa Dalloway, if they are as self-centred and shallow, their reaction takes the form of a denial of life, an attempt to escape, and leads if not to suicide then to another kind of self-destruction. This reaction takes on different disguises, but is fundamentally the same.

Mrs. Jardine's is a different case. She does not reject life; on the contrary, her greatest wish is, like Stephen Dedalus's, "to recreate life out of life"; [14] *but* it must be in her own image, whether through her own body, with her daughter, or through artistic creation. She writes a few books, which, according to her, are a great success. But neither in "direct" creation—giving birth to a child —nor in the oblique one of writing, can she reach self-forgetfulness. Everybody that crosses her path is used as a mirror in which she can see the reflection of the person she acts, the person she would have loved to be. This ethically almost satisfactory aspiration can, according to the author, serve as a valid excuse for everything Sibyl does or causes. In Rosamond Lehmann's opinion people, as it seems, are not finally to be blamed for acting the role, wearing the mask, of the sort of person they would have liked to be. The personality they act, the mask they wear has just as much claim to reality as the person who hides behind it. It should be accepted, even condoned, since it represents what they would at their best like to have been and they will suffer great pains to keep up the pretense. The flaw in this, of course, is in forgetting that life will not tolerate the imposition of theoretical constructions when they are at variance with the reality of our being. Trying to impose an artificial pattern on life invariably proves fruitless in the end. Especially if it is persisted in and enforced with vigor, life takes revenge. The greater the difference between the actual being and the act it puts on, the mask it wears, the greater the strain and so the danger of breakdown to the person behind it, not to speak of the destruction brought to others.

Mrs. Jardine could not tolerate defeat because it meant confrontation with life, with herself as she was, the woman behind the mask. She meant to be a good mother. Her craving to prove so to herself and to others is passionate just because of the internal flaw in her. She must see herself reflected favorably in the mirrors of others, finding there some constant confirmation of the reality of the person she acts—the only reality remaining to her—or else she is lost, nonexistent, and then panic sets in. As years go on and the flexibility of youth passes, she clings the more madly to the vision of herself she would impose on others. Those who are too opaque to throw back to her this apparition, who cannot be turned into accomplices, have to be converted. Unless absolutely enslaved by her charm, they represent too great a danger.

Even the innocent Rebecca, too honest and ingenuous not to pierce at moments through these disguises, has to be won over. She must be made to render back the expected reflection. Mrs. Jardine handles her as carefully as if life depended on it. Harry Jardine, on the other hand, already enthralled by her looks, her daemonic obsession in her narcissistic act, is impervious to her machinations. This is what nourishes her illusion of love for him. With him alone she can relax, sure of keeping him in thrall. But he must be handled carefully, cajoled all the time, so that he continues in uncritical admiration. She spares no effort to keep him enchanted. She puts on her finest act in his presence, for on his indifference her whole precarious personality may break into pieces. This is why she must go from success to success, from conquest to conquest; defeat must be ruled out or else she is done for.

The first and most painful defeat she suffers is the loss of her child. It is a double calamity, for she is thwarted also in her "motherhood," in her love for herself as a mother. She must keep up the illusion that this is her special vocation. A woman of strong emotions, uncontrolled in her strivings, she bitterly resents the injustice of the law that would give precedence to the father. She is thwarted as a woman. She even writes a book or two to vindicate the claims of women to achieve equality with men. There again her motive is to account for her own defeat, which she can better explain in terms of woman's subordinate position in society. The explanations she gives to the ignorant Rebecca run on the same lines. Sibyl is one of those dangerous liars—schemers may be a better word—who have an explanation for everything so convincing that it takes in themselves as well as others; who first of all are self-deceived. Their inventions are the more dangerous because masked in an apparent passion for truth. Who can see around the seeming nobility of Sibyl's fight for the rights of women, her picture of the struggle of devoted mothers deprived of the children they would have cherished and educated better than anyone else? Surely no one can understand a child better than its own mother.

Could Sibyl ever have educated Ianthe and made an independent woman of her? She would have given everything she could to her daughter—education, charm, looks; she would have made her as beautiful as possible. But what she would have created would only have been a projection of herself, for herself to admire. Ianthe would thus have been her own guarantee of existence into the future, where, in spite of herself, Sibyl knows she herself cannot reach. The more thwarted she feels in her own life, the more urgent her desire to capture her child. She lacks the most fundamental requirement for motherhood: the ability to sublimate her being in her children and to let their inclinations, the features they so early reveal, indicate the direction their own being will take, and thus to steer them through the periods of painful growth. She would have imposed her own pattern on Ianthe's life with as maniacal a force as her embittered father before her. Neither of the two was ever able to suppress their egotism and give themselves freely to the child's real potentialities. Sibyl would pour herself out in a tide of love, but she would ask everything in return. She would want her daughter's happiness only if it came through herself. It is typical of her irreducible egotism that she sends her own lover to her daughter to wean her away from the guardian to whom she has been entrusted. Motherhood, which cannot flourish unless such egotism is eliminated, has never taken root in her.

Ianthe's impulse to escape, her intuitive knowledge that her mother is her most dangerous enemy and the cause of her misery, cannot be better founded. The paranoid violence and destructiveness of her reactions are caused by her knowledge that she will not be allowed to *grow*, to become a person in her own right, to have any being apart from her mother. The events of the novel confirm these intuitions. So in the end we see that Sibyl's all but indifferent acceptance of her daughter's final alienation and confinement in an asylum—which coincides with the shock of the "betrayal" of the lover of her old age, the sculptor Gil Olafson—is entirely in character; it only completes the appalling picture we have of her. Rebecca and Gil are wrong when they decide finally that Sibyl "ought to have had a dozen." "It's what she was made for," they say. "It's all been wrong for her. She'd have been happy and glorious." [15] Not so: the evil she has sown cannot be explained away in this fashion. Far from being frustrated in motherhood, she has used motherhood to divert from herself the consequences of her failure to give herself to life. The Enchantress Queen in her dark tower of revenge, she is a source that only poisons the lives of those around her.

8

Stella Rodney

> in these last twenty of its [the world's] and her own years she
> had to watch in it what she felt in her—a clear-sightedly
> helpless progress towards disaster. The fateful course of her
> fatalistic century seemed more and more her own: together
> had she and it arrived at the testing extremities of their noon-
> day. Neither had lived before.[1]

If Elizabeth Bowen's leading motif, that of the clash
between youth and maturity, has found its best expression, and the theme of the permanent opposition of
innocence and experience a final formulation, in her
prewar novel, *The Death of the Heart* [1938], her ability
to build characters, and to render her experience of life
through these characters and their conflicts, has reached
maturity in the figure of Stella Rodney in her war novel
The Heat of the Day [1949]. Under the impact of the
war what might have taken an artist's lifetime to reach
fruition took form practically overnight. None of the
characters that have appeared in her novels since has the
completeness of this figure whose age, we notice, closely
approximates that of the author herself.

Stella Rodney is the first of Elizabeth Bowen's characters to retain innocence in spite of the experience ac-
cruing with age. Only their youth had hitherto protected
the young women and girls of Elizabeth Bowen's fiction
in their direct and spontaneous and therefore innocent
experience of life; youth alone guarded them from the
callousness of the world of the experienced, the adult,
the advanced in years. But the author's own further
growth, coinciding as it did with the outbreak of World
War II, suddenly revealed the persistence of youthful
impulses as powerful as ever and fully as intent on with-

standing the evil let loose in the world. The grimness of immediate reality brought to the author's attention the stubborn persistence of heroic virtue, however restricted its area of effectiveness might be. The stronger the pressures of evil at large, the more life is reduced to mere survival, the greater the impulse of whatever good has been planted in one's being to resist these pressures—provided one does not break under them.

Threatened by evil in innocence's last resort, one's love for another, one suddenly discovers unsuspected resources, an elemental power of resistance. In a world of victims and of destructive processes beyond control, a harmony seems still to rule events and to triumph in the end. The aristocratic author who had been fascinated by the spectacle of the breaking up of the world she was reared in, the delicate artist who used to watch intently for the cracks to appear through the smooth surface of life under the pressure of the turmoil beneath, reacts to the storm in which the whole world, all classes alike, is menaced by destruction with an affirmation of life. Stella Rodney, in whose figure and through whose destiny this vindication of life is proclaimed is therefore the most vivid character Elizabeth Bowen has ever created, just as she is a most expressive demonstration both of her author's and of the "lost generation's" idea of human personality.

Stella Rodney is almost as old as her century. Scathed by World War I, in which she lost two brothers, shipwrecked in her personal life, she imperceptibly drifts, together with her own generation, into World War II. In September, 1942, she is in London engaged in confidential work connected with the country's war effort. Her twenty-two year old son, Roderick, is in the army. In a love-affair with Robert Kelway, disabled at Dunkirk, now working in the War Office, she has found the inner harmony she had never experienced.

The constant danger of death has stimulated the dor-

mant feelings of people and created a sense of community in deserted London: "The wall between the living
and the living became less solid as the wall between the
living and the dead thinned." [2] This almost even course
of life, running like a hidden rivulet in a landscape that
might be changed out of all recognition by a chance air
raid at any time, is suddenly destroyed by the intimation,
the assertion, that her lover Robert is passing information to the enemy. The unexpected warning given by
Harrison, an odd man, almost a phantom, and at first
violently repudiated, deprives Stella of her peace of
mind. In her attempt to reassure herself that Robert is
not selling out his country, she begins to watch him
more closely, almost to spy on him. In spite of her
passionate love, her clearsightedness never deserts her.
Instead of reassurance she gets almost direct confirmation and finally Robert's personal avowal of the truth of
Harrison's statement.

Drawn close to the whirlwind of espionage and coun-
terespionage going on behind the war of battlefields,
Stella, though unprepared, manages to survive a complete breakdown in her personal life. She emerges after
her lover's death severely bruised. Tired of her single-
handed struggle with life, she looks to her son for the
protection and comfort she used to give him.

We are visually prepared for our encounter with Stella in
being led through her surroundings, the genteel part of
London she lives in, the street, the flat, the things in her
room, her clothes, and finally her own outward appearance, before we meet her directly. This oblique way of
approaching a character is deliberate and carefully
staged. It is a method initiated by Henry James, whose
Madame Merle, in *The Portrait of a Lady*, explains the
logic of it, the symbolic importance of the things we
surround ourselves with.[3] This method, giving us a, liter-
ally, substantial insight into the psyche of the characters,
is perfected in the work of Elizabeth Bowen. She in a

way took up where Henry James had left off in his
unavowed assertion of an essential human passivity in
life.[4] What he insinuated has come to be more true, or
rather has become one of the chief characteristics of the
English novel's show of life during the next half century.

Stella Rodney's greatest charm, apart from her good
looks, seems to be "the impression . . . of still being on
happy sensuous terms with life," [5] which makes her look
younger than her age. With the refinement and brilliance of a Henry James heroine, secure in her descent
from a long-established gentry, she is endowed with insight into things and people and above all with the rare
talent of looking critically into herself. Her awareness of
herself makes her an even more authentic representative
of the generation and the world she belongs to. She can
give the reader the clues directly that he would otherwise
have been at great pains to find. Her destiny blends with
that of her epoch. Her passive acceptance of things, her
inability to take action, become part of the fatalism
which seems, as if by magic, to have immobilized a
whole generation, once and forever disabled by World
War I and its aftermath. Through such a character the
history of the twentieth century, especially that of the
interwar period, acquires a human context. Why and
how the world drifted into World War II and found
itself in the midst of destruction in September, 1942,
becomes humanly understandable. To meet Stella is to
see more clearly why this world reacted to its crisis as it
did, and how it groped for a way out. With "one of those
charming faces which, according to the angle from
which you see them, look either melancholy or imperti-
nent," with her grey eyes and a "speaking set of lips," a
"complexion, naturally pale, fine, soft," with her "one
white dash, lock or wing in otherwise tawny hair . . . she
had become accustomed to being glanced at . . . Her
clothes fitted her body, her body her self, with a general
air of attractiveness and ease." [6] After her divorce, "ironically rendered almost at once unnecessary by her husband's death," [7] being left alone with her son with not

very much money, Stella was glad to be able to come to London to work after the war had broken out and while Roderick was still at school. She was "communicative and fluctuating" by temperament. "Generous and spirited, to a fault not unfeeling, she was not wholly admirable; but who is?" [8]

The failure of Stella's marriage was, like her entering into it, a consequence of the war, a consequence hastened by "her own desire to find herself in some embrace from life" which again, at that time, immediately after the war, had been a "universal" desire. She was, she knew, the "creature" of the time.

> For a deception, she could no more blame the world than one can blame any fellow-sufferer: in these last twenty of its and her own years she had to watch in it what she felt in her—a clear-sightedly helpless progress towards disaster. The fateful course of her fatalistic century seemed more and more her own: together had she and it arrived at the testing extremities of their noonday. Neither had lived before.[9]

The most prominent feature of the generation she belonged to was that of a helpless acquiescence in whatever reality presented them with. In her own life Stella followed the same pattern. Divorced by her husband, she never contradicted the story that she had divorced him. She did not mind being ostracized by her husband's family, thereby cutting her son from his closest of kin and taking, again by sheer passivity, the whole responsibility for him on herself. Her unconventional way of life, which earned her the attribute of "femme fatale," [10] a woman "capable de tout," [11] among her husband's relatives, had little to do with her actual self. She preferred this to being pitied as a woman deserted by her husband. As regards the responsibility for her son, this, if anything, stimulated her and gave meaning to her existence. Stella was not afraid of life, she was just drifting with it instead of trying to impose a direction upon it.

The most striking consequence of the first war was the

mood of indifference that set in, almost before the arms were laid down. The only protection against the shocks which endlessly followed one upon the other was to try to *feel* as little as one could. Emotional atrophy, inability to feel, led to indifference, *Gleichgultigkeit*,[12] and that again to a helpless passivity. Nothing seemed worthwhile; worse than that, nothing that one could have done, seemed to be of any use. Whatever you may do, things will take their adverse course, and the best you can do is not exert yourself. This was the disposition in which Stella's generation drifted helplessly into the disaster of World War II. Stella fully understood this disposition and—to judge by the stream of thought whose course we are allowed to follow—thought she fully shared in it. Fortunately she did not allow it to engulf the whole of her being. She saw to it that it should not affect anybody else. She was profoundly attached to her son. She also retained the ability to give herself away, to surrender in love. Then, with the coming of another war, the proximity of death and its daily heavy toll had roused people from their stupor. It had revived fellow-feelings wherever they were not fully extinct. A strong sense of community in dangers shared made strangers address each other, for "each hoped not to die that night, still more not to die unknown."[13] So Stella came to experience, during the war, a kind of love she thought she had never shared before. In this love, however, the abyss of treachery confronts her—and her story, indeed forces this question upon us: is it altogether fortuitous that the person she shares love with should have been the one of her generation, who, unlike her, has not proved able to stand the test of their times?

The result of Stella's obviously central position in the novel, and of her being cast in the role of a representative of her "lost" generation, is that all the other actors in the story in a sense derive from her. They appear to be different projections of her being, which seems to contain the

seeds of all that happens in her time and place. Elizabeth
Bowen's statement that "the relation of people to one
another is subject to the relation of each to time, to what
is happening," [14] seems to confirm this conjecture. Stella
is her own self; she is also the generation of her time, a
time of stress, of war, of all that her epoch had to go
through as its final test of survival. She and Robert, Stella
felt, "were the creatures of history, whose coming together was of a nature possible in no other day—the day
was inherent in the nature. Which must have been
always true of lovers, if it had taken till now to be seen." [15]

Robert Kelway is the one of her projections, the part
of her that contains everything that has been contami-
nated, weakened and finally ruined. By trying to rational-
ize the fall of his own generation, he has come to deny
one's belonging to one's own country, to deny, that is,
his own life. Stella for her part, though she responds
differently, is not guided by the logic of "my country
right or wrong." She follows the profounder instinct of
belonging to the soil, the conditions, that have bred her.
Of Robert she feels finally that "his denials of everything
instinctive seemed . . . to seal up love at the source." [16]
With the cold rational logic of master reason, as opposed
to the palpitating being-in-consciousness that grows from
the soil, the earth of the specific country, Robert has
unwittingly rejected her. Together with her, he has lived
for their love ever since its inception two years before,
and yet he did not understand what he was doing. His
being has suffered in adolescence, the time of the earlier
war, an early split, with two parts irretrievably disconnected. He was unable to comprehend that by betraying
the country in which he has had his being, he is betraying love. Stella knew, she almost physically felt, her
unity with living nature, the country all round, a unity
culminating in her surrender in love: "Rolled round
with rocks and stones and trees—what else is one?—was
this not felt most strongly in the quietus of the
embrace?" [17] Robert gave in at the last test. He could not
recover from defeat. The sight of the "army of freedom

queueing to be taken off by pleasure boats" [18] at Dunkirk was the last straw.

Confronted with his treachery Stella never wavers. She might find an explanation for herself; she might silently plead for him as a special case, which he undoubtedly was. Injured from birth by a monster of a mother, Robert was reared in "a man-eating house," [19] a perfect symbol, we may say, of the times. Witnessing his father's manhood being destroyed by his mother would have been enough to account for the son's weakness. Robert was, however, exposed to even greater pressure through an equally monstrous sister, the model of her mother. "It never suited them that I should be a man," [20] Robert rightly remarks. They did everything to prevent him from growing into full manhood. The argument is plausible. But never for a moment does Stella think that it has created a valid excuse for going over to the enemy, for giving up one's faith in the ultimate victory of life over death, of good over evil, at whatever cost, however meagre the immediate chances. She is one of those who, even in the autumn of 1940, in spite of all that makes her part and parcel of the "lost generation," still "could draw from some inner source" at a time "no virtue was to be found in the outward order of things." [21]

The best, the firmest part of Stella's being is projected upon her son. She tries to keep from him everything World War I and her own experience in life have violated in her. Roderick's joyful acceptance of Mount Morris, the family estate bequeathed to him by his father's cousin, appeals to Stella. She understands why Roderick should find a *habitat* for himself on the Irish estate he has never seen at a time when, with the intense sense of the timelessness of life in war, one's sense of identity had become so tenuous. The obsession with time and the times that runs like a refrain through Stella's story seems to indicate a vague sense of how one's identity might depend, and precariously, on one's continuity in time, a continuity that might, together with one's life, any minute be broken forever. Mount

Morris would give her son a firmer foothold in life and also in time. While at Mount Morris, in Ireland, a country at peace, during the war, for once free of the war's pressures, Stella realises that "the fatal connection between the past and future . . . [had] been broken before her time" and that somehow "it had been Stella, her generation, who had broken the link—what else could this be but its broken edges that she felt grating inside her soul?" [22] Yet people like herself had done their best to prevent it from breaking. She has done everything in her power not to allow the chain of continuity to get disconnected. She has not violated the allegiances that linked her to the past, so as to be able to confer them on her son intact. In the greatest crisis in her personal life, when she had to strain to the utmost her humanity, her compassion, to find an excuse for her lover and not to reject him nor deny their love, and, at the same time, accept his punishment, she did not break down. It was her clear-sightedness that helped her through the ordeal. She had the courage to see things. The greater the moment of stress, the clearer her vision.

Coming home after her last, fatal evening with Harrison which, she felt, sealed Robert's destiny, Stella explains to the inarticulate Louie, a woman at the other end of the range of womanhood in a civilized society, what the times of horror they are living through mean. "At any time it may be your hour or mine—you or I may be learning some terrible human lesson which is to undo everything we had thought we had. It's that, not death, that we ought to live prepared for." [23] The irony of it is that Louie could not possibly understand what Stella meant. Yet Stella needed just such a person to talk to, a mute witness to whom she could pour out her clear vision of the tragic hour in which ordinary people who "came into this world to see the sunlight" [24] are suddenly faced with the choice between only two alternatives: heroism or treachery. Louie's listening presence helped Stella to come sane through the crisis.

Is Louie another projection of Stella who can be used

to express her inarticulate drives, her less than fully conscious womanhood? Through the contrasting figure of Louie, Stella gains in depth. The world in which she lives acquires a broader background, a social context that is not restricted to the upper classes. Stella's lot becomes one of a vast multitude whose course is influenced by the war. But, odd though it may seem, Louie not only keeps the reader aware of the broad range of humanity alive in the war-ravaged London; her destiny touches upon that of Stella, even before they finally meet and before Stella's tragic involvement in Robert's apparently accidental death pushes Louie towards her final destiny.

Technically, Louie's part in the novel is similar to that of Septimus Warren Smith in *Mrs. Dalloway*. Left alone after her husband had joined the army, and having her parents, together with their house, swept away in Seal-on-Sea during the Battle of Britain, Louie is stunned by the war. She has no "inner source" to draw on.[25] Since she cannot find anybody to imitate she does not know what to do with herself. After she has, as she thinks, discovered that the fine lady likewise has lovers, she lets herself go. For Stella the war is a deep challenge, compelling the development of all her potentialities as a human being. She stands the test, but at the price of her personal illusions and her vitality. The war makes Louie revert to an almost subhuman level, but enables her to emerge, after she has given birth to a child whose father could hardly have been identified, with a purpose in life. The common lot of motherhood, like the common fate in which the wartime newspapers give her a sense of involvement, is something in which Louie can find an identity. From the height of life, love, and giving, Stella is hurled down never to recover completely. She emerges a subdued middle-aged woman planning a conventional marriage as a refuge from a full life of feeling and sense where she has suffered so much. Louie blunders through her life to find in the perpetuation of the species, at a time of the mass destruction of human life, a meaning for her rudimentary existence. The contrast she offers with Stella does not exhaust her role in the novel; the end of her story, like the end of Forster's *Howards End* almost forty years before, represents something general to the whole situation of England.

In her own life, her involvements, her repudiation of convention, Stella does represent her generation. She understands it and, as it seems, accepts it. Treating its members as "fellow-sufferers" [26] she cannot condemn it. But she is saved by her clear awareness of it. She has not lost her power of seeing clearly, her sense of the right and wrong of things. She might have kept her awareness at bay, but it was always there to prevent her from slipping over, giving in to the "mauvaise foi" [27] which would have meant her end. For where did the fatal *Gleichgültigkeit* it suffered from ultimately lead her generation? From refusal to feel to indifference; from indifference to loss of its hold on reality; from there to a gradual loss of identity; and finally to the inability to carry the responsibility for oneself. The complete refusal to take on any responsibility can lead either to alienation—cousin Nettie who is mad enough to have chosen a home for psychiatric cases rather than life at Mount Morris, yet sane enough to sum up in a far-reaching question the diagnosis of the malady of the age: "what is to become of us wrong ones if there's to be nobody who is right?" [28]—or it can lead in the direction taken by Robert. It leads to a loss of faith, or to the substitution of "bad faith," in either way, through a denial of one's spontaneous being that must plant its roots deep into the ground and is nourished by the love it gives and takes, ending on the side of destruction. Roderick's ready assumption of responsibility for Mount Morris should announce the advent of a new generation ready to take over, and to assert the continuity that in their own lives they felt had never broken.

9

Gulley Jimson

For everything that lives is holy. Life delights in life.[1]

Whether Joyce Cary will be remembered as a major novelist a hundred years hence may be debated. But in an essay whose goal is to try, in the context of our own times, to record both the gradual fragmentation of our conception of ourselves and the first stirrings of an attempt to make the almost disengaged parts cohere again into a stable whole, Cary cannot be neglected, whether or not his creation of whole character has fulfilled his intention. Joyce Cary, if anybody does, intentionally concentrates on character in his fiction. It was his interest in man, in individual human personality, that led him to the novel, and an exceptional ability to impersonate human character and enter into it sympathetically is fundamental to his art, which explores a remarkably wide range of cultural atmospheres, climates, ways of life based on specific ethical assumptions. His attention increasingly fixed on what was permanent in man, yet with his emotions guided by sympathy with particular examples of human suffering, he could enter into the recesses of human nature however disguised by color, place, and time. Already the figure of "Mr. Johnson" in an early novel indicates the direction in which Cary's interest will take him in his major work and suggests his latent power.

The spectacle of life with men acting their various parts became increasingly painful as the novelist advanced in years. He was not young when he began writing. When he embarked on his masterpiece, the trilogy of which the last part, *The Horse's Mouth* [1944], has been chosen to represent him in this essay, he had acquired a certain wisdom about life. The question he must repeatedly have asked himself—what makes people live in a world where injustice is the pattern of life?—was finally resolved in the realization of the inevitability of injustice, conceived dialectically as the dark side of the bright condition of human freedom. Within the natural range of human characteristics, it was this conflict of opposites that pushed mankind forward, to perhaps a new plane of being.

Three prototypes of human character are shown in his work. The first is the natural creator, most frequently a woman, who, however, if—like Sara in *The Horse's Mouth*—she does not allow convention and prejudice to divert her and lives, in Lawrencian manner, according to the laws of *being*, merges with the second, the preserver, of which Wilcher, the lawyer of the second part of the trilogy, *To Be A Pilgrim*, is representative, the more so because he is seen to be at loggerheads with the third, Gulley Jimson, the artist. This triadic explanation of humankind was only a starting point, however, for an artist of Cary's power and maturity of judgment. He was fully aware that such extreme or pure cases scarcely ever exist, that they usually combine in different proportions in one and the same person. But in his great trilogy he strictly apportions these prototypes among the three characters named because he knew, as he became absorbed in the art of fiction *per se*, that characters in fiction must be more intensely themselves than persons in reality, having—unlike characters on the stage—no physical life to give them solidity. The intensity of the novelist's art must lend them the verisimilitude of reality.

Sara, who must treacherously serve both the preserver and the artist, offers the link that keeps, in a sense, the world together. Wilcher for his part must fight the elemental artist who keeps breaking through the pattern of society that he, its preserver, feels he must uphold. Gulley Jimson, on the other hand, finds it no part of his business to consider either the problem of social continuity or the interest of the Wilchers speaking from and upholding the authority of law and order. None of the three can help being what he is, nor should he. Conflict, and therefore injustice, cannot be avoided. They are necessary and unavoidable; they are the means of progress, of the continual change that comes as a result of the collision of opposing tendencies.

Joyce Cary's intentions, embodied, as they should be in the case of an artist-novelist, in these human figures, are finally concentrated in the character of Gulley Jimson. Jimson is the most fully articulated version of the author's developing conception of what man is, or, more precisely, of what being human should feel like. Though at times this conception remains too close to the author's private heart, as one discovers in the process of analysis, nevertheless in Gulley Jimson Cary seems to have given the fullest statement to his interpretation and revaluation of man's being, and he has done so at a time most critical for man's moral survival.

Gulley Jimson has just got out of prison. He is sixty-seven. Down and out, with no money, and lacking anything that can be described as accommodations, his attention is first caught by the beauty of the scene, the sun, the Thames. All this exists to be transformed through his medium, painting, into an artifact. There is little time left, he feels he has so much to communicate in his own painter's language. Full of zest and a youthful urge to create, he begins his Odyssey in search of a studio. There is no device he would not make use of to get what he so badly needs. He does not balk at theft or blackmail so long as they prove useful. But nothing seems to work.

When he cannot express in painting the irrepressibly running stream of his consciousness of life, seized by the eye and apprehended in visual experience, Gulley must resort to words. This is not his medium, so he evokes

William Blake's lines to find a proper formulation for
what he must get out, if not on canvas then in speech.
Being a painter he finds words most unsatisfactory,
"When you're talking a lot you haven't time to get the
words right. Talk is lies. The only satisfactory form of
communication is a good picture. Neither true nor
false." [2] Without his painting gear he cannot get hold of
the form he needs and only in form can his imagination
crystallize and be released of the fruit it has borne and,
after, let the painter alone. So he grabs more fiercely for
tools, paints, and all. As a result he finds himself in
prison again, which gets him through the six autumn
and winter months. Out again, now sixty-eight, in the
fatal year 1939, his desperate reckless search finally provides him with what he needs. The running comment
with which he responds to life is relieved by periods of
creation. He paints until the end. He reaches a full
illusion of success. He is recognized by the public. His
paintings have got into the galleries. With young students from the academy that follow the great master he
paints his last and greatest wall, from which he can only
be, and is in the end, wrenched by force.

Gulley Jimson is a distinctly comic figure. Yet he is not
static or passive. He is alive and can stand his ground in
this essay, as the last in our line of figures illustrating the
changes the human personality has undergone in the first
half of this century. In this, the third of the trilogy [each
novel of which forms a complete whole and can be read
independently of the other] [3] Gulley Jimson's development from childhood to old age can be gleaned from his
sometime erratic reminiscences disclosed in his almost
unbroken running comment. It is a kind of monologue,
at times interior, more often communicated to one or
another of his friends. He lives among people devoted to
him in one of the humbler parts of London, on the
banks of the Thames. This, in terms of human landscape
probably the most colorful part of London and one that

has inspired more than one author from the times of Shakespeare, is a most appropriate background for the destitute aging tramp that Gulley Jimson has come to be. He is of the type of the "clochard," who has come to accept his status for the freedom from convention and restraint it offers. Greenbank and its surroundings will hardly let such a person starve. There is too much fellow-feeling and genuine interest in men, stimulated in Gulley's case by a sound appreciation of *genius*, which these simple people with little education unmistakenly sense.

Jimson's own description of himself, though funny, is almost cruel in its clear-sightedness. He knows the danger of self-pity, the "whore" that "gets inside you and sucks your blood," [4] so he will not indulge in it. "What offers for the celebrated Gulley Jimson? Sound in wind and limb except for arthritis, conjunctivitis, rheumatitis, sinovitis, bug bitis, colitis, bronchitis, dermatitis, phlebitis, and intermittent retention of the pee." [5] He has no illusion as to what, from a purely practical, commonsense angle, life has deprived him of. He never, for a second, insinuates that he is sorry for it; he insists, with his usual rough wit, that he "never meant to be an artist . . . I even meant not to be an artist." [6]

Gulley saw his father suffer through such a life, and his mother carry the burden of the bankrupt family. Gulley was the youngest. But he could not help it. When he got "a bad infection, galloping art," [7] he left a safe clerk's job, a wife, a baby, all the comforts, and began the life of an artist, who serves nobody but his own deamon of creation. His father had once been a most successful artist, who was on the point of being admitted into the academy when his conventional paintings that had brought him money, girls in the garden, suddenly stopped being in demand. The Pre-Rafaelites had come. Gulley's is a different case. His much more powerful artistic genius prevents him from ever stopping. The minute he has appropriated a form and exhausted the possibilities he sees in it, he must go on. His job being "always to get hold of the form he needs," [8] he cannot continue creating the postimpressionist nudes that have brought him a short-lived success. He has not exhibited, nor earned anything for fifteen years. He has lived the life almost of a beggar, relentlessly pursuing his "will of the wisp," the form that keeps eluding him. The process of creation, the sensation that he is after something real, keeps him going. The conviction that he has not yet created his greatest work, that conviction with which an artist worth his salt finally dies, drives him on and on. He keeps experimenting, developing his style.

While forced to use words instead of paints, Gulley revives the most important moments of his life, and so discloses its substance. Being an artist, he has a distinct vision of it. He sums it up for himself; in this his last phase of life and creation, he himself knows as final, and so communicates a modern artist's attitude to life that springs from his intimate experience of it. Art, as he professes, is a damnation. Except for art he would certainly not have found himself depleted in old age. But this is just a kind of lip-service to common sense, an attempt to put off the silly young idealist, Harry Barbon, referred to as Nosy, to deflect him from his own example. The young boy is infatuated with art and follows Gulley like a stray dog. Gulley for himself feels that he could not have done otherwise. He never loses sight of what this type of life, on the surface hard and obviously uncomfortable, has offered him. He never doubts the value of art, nor of his own contribution to it. Therefore there is no trace of bitterness about his own suffering, the cold, the humidity, the cramps of old age exposed to hardship beyond its power of endurance. What he does resent and tries, mostly by illicit means, to make up for is the lack of an artist's gear, paints, brushes, canvas, and some kind of studio, however modest, to appease the deamon inside him that will not let him alone.

The aged painter invades the Beeders luxurious flat and turns it into his studio, paints their wall with the Rising of Lazarus, that has been haunting him lately. He tries to get some money from Hickson, his earliest patron, who did acquire some of his best work for next to nothing but legally does not owe him anything. Gulley knows that Hickson would have been prepared to give him a subsidy if he could be sure that Gulley would leave him alone. But the artist himself admits that this would but whet his appetite for more. He puts himself into Hickson's position and, seeing himself as he is, explicitly says that the only way with people like himself is to set the police against them. Gulley's ability to look at himself critically is what keeps him fully alive. It prevents him from ever falling into self-pity. It makes him, with all his offenses against common decency, an on the whole admirable character. The crying need to break through indigence, get some cash and get to work, makes him likewise try to recover some of his old sketches from Sara, the woman with whom he lived for a time, and fought and parted; who has inspired his best work, and has been, although but briefly attached to him, all women to him.

These attempts interrupted by periods in prison, fall into the pattern of his day-to-day life. In this poorer part of London, circulating between his boat-shed and the pub, among lay preachers and prophetic, messianic craftsmen like Plantie, typical of the English world that bred Wycliffe and Blake, Gulley has his being. He is created a living character. These obscure, unknown people form the necessary human background: now Gulley's audience, now his protectors who rescue him from trouble, now his enemies trying to get the money he owes them back from him and prevent him from making a further nuisance of himself. These bystanders compose a swarming world with the unpredictable and chaotic aspect of real life that becomes comprehensible and meaningful through the presence of the artist, who both uses it for his own purposes and explains it through his art. He gives it, or rather reveals, its inherent meaning. Gulley's function in the story coincides with the role of the artist in human affairs. He discloses the inherent order in things that escapes the notice of people engaged in life on the ordinary level.

A few salient motifs gradually form out of what, at a first reading, might have seemed an aging artist's vagaries. A life rich in experience and enjoyed to its full measure has given Gulley the wisdom of old age. His artistic vision has given him the capacity to hold all his life, as though always there, in the palm of his hand all the time. Past, present, and future are simultaneously present. He does not accept the flux of time that would tie him to its inexorable course. He is free, being an artist, to live in an eternal present, to be always here and now, with no regrets to poison his delight in life, no yearning for something that might not materialize in the future. He makes the most of the living moment, trying to eternalize it in his, the artist's vision and materialize his vision in his painting. Therefore the suffering, the privations he is exposed to together with those round him, in whose life he takes a human interest, do not embitter him. They make him try to come to terms with what seems to him the core of the entire conflict of human life, the sources of misunderstanding, misery, and bitterness that lead to some final break-up of human personality.

Evoking his memories of early childhood he brings forward as a most precious gem bequeathed by his mother the idea that one should never hate. Whatever happens to one, he should not allow this feeling to nestle in his heart or else *he* will suffer the consequences, not the person he hates: "Don't hate him, Gull, or it will poison your life." [9] This timely warning that he has never forgotten runs throughout his life. It saves him from wasting himself in grievances. Provoked by cruelty, beaten up almost to death, he advises his faithful "apostle," Nosie not to allow himself to get into a state, not to wish to kill somebody, for why should one "poison . . . [one's] wells with his nasty corpse." [10]

Gulley has the author's own awareness of injustice. The conclusion he comes to is that in a world of free men whose conduct is necessarily unpredictable, justice cannot be instituted. Approximations to it will continue to be attempted, but how can you discipline a free being and subordinate it to an imposed pattern? On the other hand, freedom itself is the precondition of existence on a human level. There could be no progress without it and, above all, no art. Without art mankind would stagnate. For the artist eternalizes the living moment. By giving it a form imagination embodies its being. Once it has acquired its form, its utterance, it becomes an autonomous influence that keeps mankind alive to its own existence. The artist is free to continue his eternal search after new forms into which to pour and communicate the vision without which mankind could not see itself as it is and so could not be aware of itself as being. Why then should one resent the injustice in life and allow "that sense of justice" [11] to destroy one, to prevent one from enjoying life? The meaning of life is life: "Life delights in life." [12] Once one has understood it with the whole of one's being, he can enjoy life. He can shed the unnecessary conventions and fit his existence to his "being," in a Lawrencian sense; adapt it to the central drive he feels within him and be harmonious.

Gulley offends conventions. The only authority he respects is the one imposed by creation. Everything else is subject to that. The women he loved were put into the service of his art. Sara, the "eternal woman," who keeps building her nest, however often it may be destroyed, in a sense "nails him down upon a rock—Catches his shrieks in cups of gold." [13] She, the elemental mother and wife, attracted Gulley more powerfully than any other. Their contrasting creative urges collided. He would not allow her to make use of him, to build her nest and satiate her thirst for family, complete with the man. He would not burn out his creative flame in carnal embrace. She would subdue his daemon, make him serve their hearth, and pour both his and her own creativeness into day-to-day enjoyment of life in lust. They must clash. Moments of purest, profoundest joy in each other as man and wife, always innocent through being always new, alternate with fierce conflict: the physical resistance of the little man, the artist, against the big mother-wife. The restless artist must go on, destroy whatever stands in his way of creating new forms. The mother-wife would make him father of her children, eldest son, provider, keeper of the nest she must go on rebuilding.

Every woman Gulley loved had in turn to be subdued, subordinated to his creative genius. Once completely enslaved they could no longer inspire him and so they could not give him anything. His search continued. He did not bring any of them much happiness; they were victims rather than partners with whom he could set up the joy of life against the suffering exacted in payment. Sara was the only one to be equal to him. She followed as fearlessly her incontrollable *self* as he did. She sinned against many laws and rules, but never against what really mattered in life. So she could retain harmony, equanimity, and joy of life in the face of adversities. The only thing she could not accept was old age, physical decay, the loss of her vitality, and her looks and charm. Her delight in life depended so much on physical resources, on the human body, that she could not get reconciled to their irretrievable loss or to the irreversible passage of time. But aging did not bother Gulley, whose creative imagination could carry him beyond the border of human life and into eternity.

In the end before his death Gulley does find his wall; "happy fortune reserved the best for my last—the last love of my old age . . . the crowning joy of my life." [14] He tries to pour all the experience of his life on it. Dukes and duchesses haunt the famous artist's decrepit chapel to order portraits. The comic Alabaster, just as much of a tramp as Gulley, writes his biography: *The Life and Works of Gulley Jimson*. He follows him about to get wisdom straight from "the horse's mouth." [15] Gulley now has a kind of school of his own. Twelve young students from the academy work under his guidance at

the enormous wall painting. A rapidly drawn imitation
of his early best work, of the Sara period, provides him
with the money. His dream seems to have come through.

But just as the old rascal expects, something will fall
on his head before he is through. The old chapel is
falling into ruins. The authorities warn Gulley, they try
to talk him away from it. But how can he give up now
that the daemon of creation has him tight by the throat?
As though infected by a creative fever, he and his young
crowd work day and night. Gulley has a sense of completeness. His whole life seems to fall into a pattern. He
is putting his vision on the wall exactly as he sees it with
his inner eye. Just then he learns that Sara had died in
hospital as a consequence of the blow he had inflicted on
her while trying to get the drawing he has copied away
from the old cheat. In his last night in the chapel while
drawing the whale's eye—it is the creation, not the fall,
with which he will take his leave of life—Sara appears to
the delirious artist. In a colloquy with her he goes
through what was best in his life. They almost renew
their old quarrel, but now in a subdued way, both beyond the limits of bitterness.

Art, according to Sara, has spoiled the sweet life they
might have had. They were so perfectly fitted for each
other, and knew so well how to relish life. But Gulley
understands the dialectics of it. He knows that it was
just the driving genius in him that has taught him how
to squeeze the most out of their best moments. These
moments could not last. The consummation they led to
had to be passed on to the immortal artifacts they inspired. Just this, the eternal reaching out after something
one can never attain, has made them immortal. She
reproaches him for his service to art instead of to love, to
herself. She insists that this last attempt, Gulley hanging
in the cradle above ground and working with fever rising,
will kill him. He knows she is right, just as he knows that
he cannot help it. This is what he was made for. This is
where everything she enjoyed in him came from, everything that, making their life happy and harmonious,

precluded it from continuing for long. She must jealously follow him and try to win him over from his art and from other women. He must serve his art, perpetually follow his artistic vision and transform it into a solid form. This is why he can accept his artist's lot: his life and his death. She could not help becoming the "alma mater" Gulley reproaches her with being: "There you go, Sall, you old bluemange, you've thrown away your stays at last and taken the whole world to your bosom." [16] She cannot help being sorry that she is dead and that life is gone. He has all his life in the present moment, therefore he cannot regret the past. He has eternity through art, so he can accept his death. She can't help asking herself the same question over and over again: "why can't people be happy, poor dears? Why do they have to go moiling and toiling and worrying each other? Life's too short." [17] Gulley is profoundly shaken by her death. He is sorry that he is "done for," [18] but he realizes that this is "the way things are" [19] and he as an artist "ought to know what life is." [20] He must go back to work, there is so little time left. Tears run down his cheeks, he can hardly retain his sobs, life without Sara seems unthinkable, but "putting another touch on the old 'un's nose, to give it more elevation [is] Practically A MATTER OF LIFE AND DEATH, you might say, or thereabouts." [21]

Gulley Jimson is one of those figures who have appropriated a whole gamut of human character. He is what a character in fiction, according to Marcel Proust, must be: a complex creation in which many living models have become fused. He comes as his author's ultimate vision of what man is and what he should be to delight in life. Cary presents him to the reader at a time he himself must have come to Gulley's conclusions on life, probably at just as high a price. The painter had to come into conflict with law and order and its preservers. Wilcher the lawyer is therefore most unfavourably interpreted by Gulley:

men like Wilcher . . . frighten me. They're not normal. You never know what they'll do next. They're always fit for rape and murder, and why not, because they don't look upon you as human. You're a Lost Soul, or a Bad Husband, or a Modern Artist, or a Good Citizen, or a Suspicious Character, or an Income Tax Payer. They don't live in the world we know, composed of individual creatures, fields and moons and trees and stars and cats and flowers and women and saucepans and bicycles and men: they're phantoms, spectres. And they wander screaming and gnashing their teeth, that is, murmuring to themselves and uttering faint sighs, in a spectrous world of abstractions, gibbering and melting into each other like a lot of political systems and religious creeds.[22]

Gulley could not possibly come near to understanding the preserver, being himself the artist-creator made to destroy in order to create. There is nothing to draw him to a Wilcher, who, on his side, can have nothing but suspicion, or loathing, for such as Gulley.[23] Wilcher must save society from destruction at the hands of the artist, who, living in the eternal present, might cut himself off from any moorings and so, while trying to eternalize his own and his kind's moment in time, for "eternity is in love with the productions of Time," [24] break up the indispensable continuity of ordinary life. Jimson's function is to keep men like Wilcher on their guard and, like "a little mosquito biting a big public behind," [25] keep them alive.

By serving art and allowing nothing to divert him from his course, Gulley Jimson does what he is made to do; therefore he maintains his inner harmony. This saves him from giving way to bitterness, from getting up a grievance that would kill him as it did his father, who both feared exploring new forms, and so denied his creative genius, and broke down as though poisoned when he was rejected by the public. One's bitterness really comes from one's dissatisfaction with oneself projected upon life. At the end of his life Gulley understands and preaches with a passionate articulateness that art is the yeast of life, that by "holding the mirror up to nature" art keeps mankind aware of itself and rejuvenates it:

What keeps it moving is not a big public shoving its little foot forward, but a little mosquito biting a big public behind. If you left the world to itself . . . it would die of fatty degeneration in about six weeks. It would lie down in the nice rich mudbank where it finds itself and close its eyes and stuff its ears and let itself be fed to death down a pipe-line. But God, not intending to lose a valuable pedigree hog that way, has sent a mosquito to give it exercise, and fever and the fear of death.[26]

Gulley also realises the all-important function of the individual—so sorely neglected in the twentieth century, which, overwhelmed by the task of caring for everyone in vast human communities, neglected the living individuality of each of them. In his grotesque way, comic in its exaggerations while metaphorically true, Gulley ridicules "the Economic Man brainless, eyeless, wicked spawn of the universal toad sitting in the black bloody ditch of eternal night and croaking for its mate which is the spectre of Hell." [27] He laughs at the widely held idea that man as an individual does not matter, but is to be treated as member of a class, a profession, a group, a category. Relying upon man in the mass, an amorphous collectivity, to achieve progress seems absurd to the aging artist. Modern history has shown that the mass, consisting of individuals, can accomplish something only if the level of each of the individuals in it is brought to a certain standard. The cultivation of the individual has again proved essential.

Art, like imagination, is eternal. It cannot be suppressed. The obscure unschooled men of the Greenbank world help it in their warm human way and so keep the genius of the nation alive. The rich ones patronize it, while trying to protect their property. Gulley keeps no grudge against them. Let us be clear about what this attitude means. The implication is not that all is for the best in the best of worlds and that classes should be maintained at all cost. The implication is that progress will come through the growth of the individual in whose formation art should play a leading role. Gulley's life has been useful. He has enjoyed it. He has become invulnerable early in life. Art has helped him to suppress self-pity, it has saved him from bitterness. Being a creator he cannot hate: "Walls have been my salvation, Nosy . . . Walls and losing my teeth young, which prevented me from biting bus conductors and other idealists. But especially walls." [28] He has understood the eternity of life, of man who, like D. H. Lawrence's phoenix, rises from his ashes, his fall having given him the chance of resurrection. If a man follows his being, he enjoys life, becomes one with it and delights in it. He has also understood that hatred and bitterness are destructive. And above all he has through personal experience discovered that there is no reason for grievance; the privilege of being alive is itself the source of beauty, truth, goodness, harmony.

"It is dangerous for you to talk, you're seriously ill,"— the nun warns Gulley while in the police ambulance on the way to the hospital. "I should laugh all round my neck at this minute if my shirt wasn't a bit on the tight side." "It would be better for you to pray." "Same thing, mother." [29] So the best praying, the contemplation of deity that should bring man into harmony with the universe, is laughter, the loud glorification of life.

Gulley, representing, as it appears, mankind at grips with the monster of destruction—the approaching war runs like a kind of subdued leitmotif throughout the novel, set in 1938–39—ends his life with a loud affirmation of life. He has come to accept and enjoy it not because he has kept it at bay, but because he has learnt to know it inside out and has come out of the scuffle undefeated: "A man is more independent that way, when he doesn't expect anything for himself." [30] For, as his favorite poet—old Billy, William Blake, had discovered so long ago—life is its own reward: "Everything that lives is holy. Life delights in life." [31] If one is able to live up to it, he will find his happiness even in life's adversities.

10

Reprise

By the time we come to the end of our investigation of the English novel in the first half of our century we realize with a shock that the progressive disintegration of the life of human personality, a process one hoped to see completed, has not yet run its full course. From the early signs of the breaking up of the firm ground under the feet of character in fiction at the turn of the century to the determined if futile attempts to maintain a basis for life in a world crumbling under the impact of the most destructive of wars more than fifty years later, the steady process of dissolution seems to have continued unchecked. The corrosive process that affected Conrad's Lord Jim has gained momentum by the time of D. H. Lawrence's Ursula, and rises to a new peak of intensity under the merciless eye of such intransigent humanists as James Joyce and Virginia Woolf, until in the degraded figures created by Graham Greene and Evelyn Waugh and in the self-deluded and destructive mother-figure of Rosamond Lehmann's novel we come, as it seems, to the very sources of decomposition. A recovery begins, within severe limits, during—significantly—the tumult of World War II in the painful effort of Elizabeth Bowen's Stella Rodney to recapture stability and in the figure of Joyce Cary's Gulley Jimson—though just at the moment when one wants most to believe that man can transcend the shattered present and, reaching out through art into eternity, recreate a vision of himself that points to salvation in reality, the transcending creation, the great work of art, is itself destroyed before it is fully created, and the vision dissolves in a dying man's choking words.

What the reader has gained by watching the depressing scene of dissolution can best be demonstrated if one attempts to sum up what each of the characters has disclosed, i.e., what each of these novelists has contributed to our better knowledge of ourselves, which in the final analysis is what art, and only art at its best, can offer. In assessing what it is that Jim, Ursula, Stephen, Clarissa, and all the successive figures have communicated to a reader eager to understand the age he lives in and so to penetrate into his own being and come to terms with the world he confronts, we find that we can treat them as contemporaries, as coexisting with ourselves, further removed though we may be in time. That we can do so points to the power and quality of the new insights into man each of the artists here dealt with has contributed in the character he has built. The fact that what these characters have to offer is as new now as it was at their making is the best proof imaginable of the originality of their creators' work and of the value and authority of the art, the fictional tradition, through which they have their being.

Jim's refusal to accept the dark side of his personality, his striving after unrealistic ideals, the destructive persistence of his youthful illusions, symbolizes for Conrad the lot of mankind: "And yet is not mankind itself, pushing on its blind way, driven by a dream of its greatness and its power, upon the dark paths of excessive cruelty and excessive devotion? And what is the pursuit of truth, after all?"[1] Marlow's repeated "he was one of us" is there to remind the reader that Jim stands for all mankind. He represents the human figure in its fragility, which is in the first place inward and psychological. The rich human imagination stimulates a perpetual tendency to live in a world of dreams. The conscious mind cannot control this, just as it cannot control man's irrational drives. There is not only the doubleness of man's nature, with two forces, dark and bright, constructive and destructive, forever fighting for possession of man's soul; there is also the refusal to mature, to accept life and oneself on their own terms.

Human character has come to seem too complex to fit the older rationalist conception of man, with its optimism about his character and progress. We find ourselves, and our lives, far more difficult to understand and control. Our common ideas of good and bad, right and wrong, do not always have the same resonance in the innermost human personality. "We are snared into doing things for which we get called names, and things for which we get hanged, and yet the spirit may well survive—survive the condemnations, survive the halter, by Jove! And there are things—they look small enough sometimes too—by which some of us are totally and completely undone." [2]

The picture of human character that rises from the pages of *Lord Jim* looks in disarray. That complex portrait of man given us by modern psychology here emerges nearly complete. By the board go all certitudes about the fundamental goodness of human nature, and in particular the myth of the natural man, the "noble sauvage" inevitably virtuous while living in nature but depraved by the iniquitous conditions of an unjust civilization. The idea that by giving everybody the same chance everyone will be good and happy, the doctrine of character underlying the doctrine of progress, is exposed.

With Jim the reader is presented with a more truthful image of man: his internal conflict between his good and his bad potentialities reflecting the conflict between himself and the world. His special plight is that, though he is in possession of consciousness and knows much, he does not know enough. His poetic imagination draws its power from the irrational, that realm of being ignored by the liberal tradition though recovered by psychoanalysis. Men's fantasies, whose promise of future progress leads mankind on, are shown to be responsible for more trespassing of the law, more suffering and tragedy, than people would like to admit—just as they are responsible for those imaginative flights into the universe beyond our own that are open to man alone. The cosmos outside us is reflected in the no less inscrutable cosmos within us: "The human heart is vast enough to contain all the world. It is valiant enough to bear the burden, but where is the courage that would cast it off?" [3] The full range of human potentialities, as Conrad saw them at the turn of the century, far outstrips the moral power of man's personality, the courage he needs to carry the burden they entail.

Skepticism or suspicion about the existing order was by no means instinctive to Conrad, nor was the habit of claiming special allowances for human frailty. But he served his art as uncompromisingly as did Henry James and gave free play to his artist's imagination, that at the last does not respect any laws or limits but its own. Therefore, to his surprise and sometimes indignation,[4] he created characters that, simply in being true to life, undermine the foundations of liberal-rationalist tradition. The stable individual figure, potentially heroic, begins to dissolve. The "Irrational that lurks at the bottom of every thought, sentiment, sensation, emotion," [5] hitherto unheeded, begins to penetrate to the surface. It catches the attention of those who are able to see and have the courage to admit what they have seen. Yet, knowing the worst, those artists, possessing such courage could continue to hope, as artists, for the best, realizing that even with the destructive darkness within him, or perhaps just because of it, man can and must aspire to the stars in order simply to keep going, to survive on a level above that of the brutish animal. It is the plight of modern man to see that, while searching for a way that would lead to the stars, he is constantly pulled down by forces of darkness which would make even the most routine and pedestrian existence an inescapable dilemma.

Why is it, we may ask, that Ursula Brangwen, as a character in fiction, in the final analysis does not quite satisfy? Is it possibly just because of the author's extraordinary emphasis on her inner being, an emphasis which in his own view should have made her more real? Understanding that her conscious *ego* must derive from the unconscious, Lawrence shows Ursula acting out of character, in unpredictable ways, but in so doing he only heightens her verisimilitude. His presentation of her adds genuine novelty and freshness to the picture of human character formed in the modern novel. But what makes her at the same time less than wholly complete is the author's concentration on this one inward aspect of her being to the exclusion at times of everything else in life. Feeling the urgency of her problem as a woman of joining her being to that of another, a man, he ends by separating her from everything else in the community, in the world around her. The impression finally created is that this isolation is due not only to her temporary obsession with herself in her attempt to resolve her fundamental relatedness to life through union with another. One rather gets the impression that Ursula lacks the capacity to go beyond this one relation and join the common world. This, instead of lending her a broader universality, makes her almost a special case, which is obviously not what the author intended.

By taking for his terms of reference the internal man, and for his field of exploration the unknown unconscious, D. H. Lawrence seems to have lost touch with the external personality, which the internal depends on as much as it forms and supports. The question which of the two counts for more in the human equation seems irrelevant. The external world, in which the outer personality finds its form, became an almost abstract notion to Lawrence. It lost the attributes of a living world. It became a cipher in his imagination, a vehicle for his indictment of a civilization that he saw as governed by abstract intellect, subjected to impersonal will, and drifting steadily towards self-destruction. So, too, after being plunged into her own inner being to find the image that will be reflected in the man she can love, Ursula herself begins to change into a vehicle through which the perpetual but impersonal rhythm of life's pulsation steadily beats; her individual outlines get more and more blurred. On both sides the prophet outvoices the creative artist and impairs his creation—the character. The artist's concern should be Ursula, not his message—and then both Ursula and the message would have got through. The prophet's counsel was to follow the being, not the mind. But under the decisive force of his obsession, the being itself loses its natural unity; it, too, falls apart.

In Joyce's Stephen and in Joyce himself, for the author can hardly be separated from the character he created, is telescoped the spiritual crisis of modern European civilization. Through his rejection not only of religion but of family, country, everything that tied him to his early life and rooted him in history, and through the great task he sets himself of finding his own ground, creating his own habitat, Stephen tests as an artist the nineteenth-century conception that man in and of himself is strong and stable and has a natural right to full moral and intellectual freedom. Once emancipated, he can achieve everything; there are no limits to his possibilities. This attitude permitted Joyce to take full responsibility for himself. More than that it stimulated him to set himself apart from mankind, allowing no suspicions to undermine his faith in the power of human personality. So he set out on his long search: "To discover the mode of life or of art whereby your spirit could express itself in unfettered freedom."[6] Yet his mode of reasoning, his habits of thinking and acting, continued not only Irish but Jesuitic, tending increasingly towards—and deriving power from—ritualistic and sacramental acts. The unconditioned life he so warmly welcomed at the end of his adolescence—"Welcome, O life!"—escaped him. He was ultimately lost in a maze of archemotifs, myths, and legends, submerged in another ritualistic all-language.

James Joyce's Stephen, especially in the stages that follow the *Portrait* [but were already anticipated there] is a distinctive case of *disintegration* in human personality. In the moral and intellectual confusion of the early part of this century and through the twenties, a writer of Joyce's acute perceptiveness, his sensibility resounding to the slightest vibrations in the "atmosphere of the mind" —if we may again resort to Henry James's fount of literary terminology—could but go on exploring, analysing, and thus fragmenting, in a frantic search after the meaning things seemed to have lost. An artist of unequalled power, his genius could express itself only by taking things apart. In his insight very much ahead of his time, as a personality he was not ready to concede what he had discovered in man. Therefore he could not build a full human figure who would be both true to the divided nature of man yet also strong enough to meet the challenge of the coming dark ages.

In the grim decade following on the First World War, the greatest watershed in the modern history of the West, the figure of Clarissa Dalloway stands as a symbol of the psychosis that was spreading like a disease through the nerve-centers of society. Clarissa's rejection of her own "being" [7] is typical of the history of the so-called "lost" generation and of the profound, paralysing fear of reality that had come to them, prematurely, with the brutal shock of the war. With all her long-nurtured refinement of feeling, Clarissa finally comes to the same conclusion as H. G. Wells's Mr. Polly twenty years before, the poor, awkward, ungrammatical little man at the other pole of English society. Mr. Polly was sure he would return, even after he was dead, to the beautiful spot in the garden to watch the sun set: "Come here always when I'm a ghost . . . I'd be a sort of diaphalus feeling—just mellowish and warmish like." [8] So Clarissa believed that she would survive "somehow in the streets of London, on the ebb and flow of things, here, there . . . she being part, she was positive, of the trees at home . . . being laid out like a mist between the people she knew best, who lifted her on their branches as she had seen the trees lift the mist." [9]

Give up your *self*, your conscious being and the responsibility it involves, and rejoin nature—this is where Polly's search has led him. He accepts it. Only on the unconscious level after the death of your *self* can you commune with others—or on an animal level, as Virginia Woolf says in her last novel, *Between the Acts* [but could not accept]. On the conscious level you are isolated, you are alone. Human nature is against you to punish you for not feeling and therefore denying reality. As a consequence reality escapes you. You may regain it only if you are ready to accept together with its glamor, harmony and beauty, its darkness, squalor, ugliness, deformity, the smell of the lower classes—the Miss Kilmans who perspire [10]—that is, only if you modify your aesthetic view of things, give up your social superiority, your privileged isolation, and change.

Could Mrs. Dalloway change? She could not. Therefore the only escape was death. But one should put it off as long as one can. "Assemble" as many people as one can, supply life from the outside, the multicolored crowd. Fill one's kaleidoscopic mind with bits and ends gleaned by one's impressionist-painter's delight in nature and things, one's glimpses into things and people. You should not try to synthesize, because you will fail. You can survive so long as you can "assemble" your dispersed personality, bits of it with Peter, others with Sally, some with Richard, a flattering apparition of yourself in your daughter Elizabeth, for you do not exist by yourself; there is nothing but void in you, you exist in these acquiescent others. One day you may no longer be able to "assemble," to rejoin the party and mix however superficially with life; then darkness will overwhelm you. The dread of life, the terror of death, will irresistibly draw you towards your only liberation in death. Septimus Warren Smith's suicide, like a death knell, resounds in the depths of Clarissa's mind, to be hushed, ignored, suppressed, never eliminated, and it will drive her eventually into suicide.

Where did the search for an authentic personal reality, more real than the one cultivated by the documentary realists, ultimately lead Virginia Woolf? Reality contained in moments of vision permanently escapes the artist. With it goes his hold on life. The author draws apart; loneliness closes on him. The outside world becomes dim; it gets obliterated and vanishes. The author turns to its reflection in the mind, but can the reflection hold its shape if its source is denied? Can any character continue alive if its ambience, the "medium" in which it exists, is ignored? The split between oneself and the world penetrates into one's own being. It runs right through one's centre and one's personality begins to break up. Then "human nature with red nostrils" [11] comes up against you to punish you for ignoring it. The only escape from it is death. The world of the 1930's, of 1939 and after, with masses of humanity systematically driven into death, looms very near—and the image of man given us by the modern novel seems more and more a prophetic warning.

Does it make any real difference whether Tony Last is alive or dead? If it was not for the memorial stone, who would have remembered him? Nobody shed a tear for him. He had never lived, so he could never die, as a man. Mrs. Dalloway, haunted by her fear and refusal of life was driven by a wish for death, for only through death might she realize that she had been alive. But the degraded Lasts have fallen so low that they are unaware of life, of themselves as living, so they cannot even be aware of the fear of life in them. Dead in life, they cannot *die*. The only punishment that can be meted out to them is to make them *live*.

In these terms the end of A *Handful of Dust* seems an anticipation of Sartre's *No Exit*. Tony Last is still physically alive but he is existentially dead because, now that he has got the taste of what life might have been, he is denied the affirmative act through which he might have asserted himself as a living being and escaped the hell of being buried alive. The meaning is the same. The "néant" has opened its jaws ready to swallow the man who refuses to commit himself to life. The only difference seems to be that the metropolitan Frenchman has given his creatures the ambience of an urbane hotel, while the gentleman-imperialist Englishman found in the waste of a jungle and a lifetime of genteel enslavement reading Dickens, a more adequate surrogate for hell.

What is hard to settle, however, is how far this debased human being can be treated as representative of the various transformations to which the conception of human personality was subjected in the first half of our century, or rather in the negative interwar period. The author's insinuation, contained in the name *Last*, would mean that Tony belongs to the receding past, that his social background, his ways of life, together with the ill-fated end it led to, is something departing this world. If so, we can only be relieved, through pitying. For Tony and his kind, however historians may rate their actual importance in bringing to pass the catastrophes of our century, have been thoroughgoing accomplices in the drift that produced them and tolerated their coming. Tony's unconscious destructiveness, his horribly casual *degradation*, corresponds finally to the way in which, lost in a maze of pseudo-beliefs and abandoned allegiances, the uprooted world of modern Europe drifted to its doom—the horrors of World War II—with nobody, as it seemed, trying to prevent it.

Faced with human depravity abroad and in himself, Scobie tries to escape. In the critical thirties, when politics was imposed on the attention of everybody by the course events had taken in Europe, people like Scobie refused the challenge. But the result of a refusal to commit oneself at a time when reality has reduced the choice to the bare extremes—life or death—is that if you are not on the side of life, you are on the side of death.

By his passivity Scobie decided for death: "We are all of us resigned to death: it's life we aren't resigned to." [12] Such an attitude to life leads to one's own destruction as a final solution.

The neurosis that spread in the thirties, with its prophetic obsession with the man-hunt and the persecution *raisonnée*, is condensed in the crisis of Scobie's life. He is rent by an internal conflict expressed in the two voices in him: one points to a way out, the other and louder one to an *impasse*. His own disposition makes him more liable to the life-denying neurosis. Scobie's mind is more open to the influences abroad than that of earlier generations who had a stable community with firm beliefs and attitudes to fall back upon. Deprived of that support, he looks for a metaphysical basis in Catholicism, but cannot find it there. He tries to understand people through love, but since he does not love himself, he cannot love. His meagre vitality soon exhausted, he cannot resist the seemingly malevolent reality of his life. He identifies the whole of life, the whole of the world, now and hereafter, with his own failure and is lost in loneliness.

Scobie has not the power to look at things beyond the span of a human life and so he cannot find comfort in the realization that the present is only a brief, dark period in human history, not all there is in life. He identifies the universe with his own lot, and imposes his own misery on it to justify his self-pity: "If one knew, he wondered, the facts, would one have to feel pity even for the planets? if one reached what they called the heart of the matter?" [13] What remains to a man who has cut life and the hereafter, the lot of all mankind, down to his own paltry measure? Scobie has never trusted love or life, and life never trusts him. The ultimate salvation he expected to achieve through religion, which he adopted as a rampart against an unacceptable world, that salvation for which he pleaded in his last words: "Dear God, I love . . ." [14] could only fail him once he had refused in his miserable egotism of fear and self-pity to obey the

Commandments and so burnt the bridges behind himself.

The figure of Major Scobie sums up the degradation of man reduced to such an obnoxious state of being that his greatest problem is no longer how to live and enjoy life, but how to get rid of the life that was imposed on him; how to depart unobserved, and prevent others from suffering for him, since his whole existence has become reduced to inflicting pain while trying to alleviate it. There can be no darker vision of life. In English literature until 1950, I think, the negative attitude to life, the denial of human values and man's dignity, reached its climax in the destiny of Major Scobie. His death; the posthumous loathing of his widow, who tries to denigrate him; the degradation of Helen, driven into promiscuity through her experience with Scobie; Ali's death, that comes as Sobie's reward for fifteen years of devoted service—all make his life appear to have been not only unnecessary, but positively harmful. The reader is invited to draw the most pessimistic conclusion on the value of human existence, a conclusion that the Second World War hardly permits us to controvert.

With Mrs. Jardine this inquiry reaches into one of the central conditions of personal existence, which nevertheless somehow seems continuously bypassed in fiction— the condition of motherhood and the question of a woman's innate incapacity for this role. Nobody is responsible for the fact that the inclination to give freely is not given to everybody and that not every woman is a born mother, but we can all be held responsible for ignoring this fact. Mothers like Mrs. Jardine abound.

Sibyl Jardine reflects one of the most typical deficiencies in the human makeup. She shows another facet of the same deeply rooted fear of life, an innate insecurity which does not allow her simply to *be*. She is the archetype of the monster-mother figure which accounts for the disintegration of the family at the source, for the withering away of young lives before they are able to emancipate themselves and build their own lives. Wreathed in lies, surrounded with adulation, elevated to the throne of the Holy Virgin, this mother figure is responsible for countless victims nipped in the bud. Such women usually enjoy not only confidence but the reputation of being mothers *par excellence*. People are taken in by the virtuoso act they put on: the more deficient in motherhood, the more virtuosity in the act. And yet, as it appears, more of misery, mental aberration, and suffering is due to such mothers than people would like to admit. The public support given them makes it almost impossible for the young victims to break through and get protection against them.

Here, at the source, the dissolution of personality begins. The mother who through self-effacing love should stimulate the young into being, driven by daemons of her own unfulfilled personality, destroys her own children. The sooner the fallacy of the universal sanctity of motherhood is seen through the better. The sanity of countless unprotected children and adolescents depends on it. One could almost say that the soundness of generations to come largely depends on the desecration of this destructively idealized mother figure and the substitution for it of the genuine, real woman, who is either capable of spontaneously giving love in motherhood or, if not, brave enough to see it and responsible enough not to cause as much evil as Sibyl Jardine and her like have done. For wickedness in one generation, or rather the suffering caused by such wickedness, may cause, and often does, madness in the next. If we look for the sources of the disintegration of personality so frighteningly revealed in this investigation we should not overlook this, maybe the most important one—the inviolate mother figure no law courts, or public bodies, are brave enough to attack.

Among the characters we have examined it is Elizabeth Bowen's Stella who, at the price of her private emotional life, tried to keep the chain of human continuity from breaking. Her repudiation of her generation's indifference in her denial of her lover once he is found out to be a traitor represents her personal contribution to the moral stability so essential for those who are to succeed. Her son may therefore be able to inherit Mount Morris and maintain its actual and its symbolic value; what she has done may help to prevent the flame of individual being from being extinguished.

Stella points a way out which to a Clarissa Dalloway, a Tony Last, or a Major Scobie would have seemed an *impasse*. Her involvement in the time and world in which she lives and to which she acknowledges her allegiance saves her from the internal void, the isolation and the self-pity, that ravage these others. Brave enough to see herself as she is, she escaped the dehumanizing fatality that, under different disguises, led her generation to self-destruction. Instead of spreading decay by trying to vindicate her failure in marriage through her son, as a Sibyl Jardine would have done, she gave her son her love so simply and completely that she could turn to him in her need once the spring of her own revival, through Robert's love, had been sealed for her.

After accomplishing the essential human function her fatalistic, irresponsible generation had refused, Stella withdrew into passivity, a conventional marriage. She had done what she could to prevent the succession from breaking and leaving the new generation in midair. Her story represents an early attempt to conceive the reintegrating of human personality, however damaged, bruised, and reduced it was by the ordeals of the two Wars and the demoralizing, rotting influence of the morbid interwar period.

Is Gulley Jimson as a figure in fiction strong enough to carry the burden of the affirmation of life Joyce Cary intended?

After the reader has assimilated what Gulley has to communicate he may come to the conclusion that Gulley himself, on whose compactness the forcefulness of his glorification of life depends has in the process spent himself in words. He does sum up and in a sense re-collect the splintered bits and ends of the liberal tradition of consciousness and morality with which this essay unintentionally opened. The sheer effort to reconfirm his shaken creed seems, however, to have deprived Gulley of his physical existence. To make his statements persuasive the author himself has to step in. In the end Gulley becomes a voice, the voice of reason, of humanity, and of an all-embracing pity for and acceptance of man as he really is, now that both appearance and reality, façade and substance, the good and the bad, have been revealed. Cary's determination to hope against hope, to believe in spite of doubt, and to express a self-imposed faith in the loud glorification of life by the dying artist, does not, after some consideration, seem wholly effective. The novelist has been defeated in his effort to recreate in this character a full human figure in the tradition of the early picaresque novel, which, while deriving its power from the Renaissance moral consensus, maintained its existence for a time in the face of that oncoming rationalistic idealism that would deprive it of its lifelikeness, its all-round unashamed truth to life.

Joyce Cary, too, seems to join the artists who scoured the obscure territory of our century in search of human personality that should have persisted intact from time out of memory to the present age. He could conceive of a stable human figure on the level of the elemental woman, such as Sara Monday; but with Tom Wilcher words begin to take over, finally submerging the lawyer into his class and his time and losing his individuality instead of reaffirming it. Under the pressure of the author's ambition Gulley himself is transformed before the end of the novel into words that flow uncontrollably from him. The figure created in him has in the end to be artificially kept together by means of various repetitive devices while the torrent of words runs uninhibited throughout the narrative. We remember the argument, the author's testament, most articulately rendered in this, Cary's most ambitious novel; we doubt only the character made to speak it.

In trying to reconfirm the value of man, to consolidate the shattered human personality, Cary disobeyed the rule he set himself in the case of Sara Monday, as stated in the author's own prefatory essay, the rule of "character first." [15] What Gulley has to convey to the convulsed world on the eve of World War II is given precedence, the ideas Cary thought he had to impart, and this detracts from the roundness of Gulley's figure. For all his lifelikeness Gulley is eventually sacrificed to the author's message. Since it is the importance of the individual that he has to reassert and through it the novelist's belief in the dignity of man, by losing substance as character Gulley fails in his mission. Instead of counteracting the fragmentation of human personality Cary himself finally becomes its victim.

The most one can claim is that Gulley marks another attempt, more distinct and maybe more determined than that realized in Stella, to save, reassemble, reintegrate the human figure at a time that was not yet propitious for such a feat. The odds were against the artist. The message he invested in the figure of Gulley Jimson revealed the author hiding backstage. Cary in person could not at the time—[1944]—securely reassess human values. Man was to be subjected to yet another severe test. The atomic bomb was to be loosed against the world before man could embark on a search of his own identity which should ultimately lead to the slow process of a moral revival.

This essay, conceived in the belief that the re-integration of man was near at hand, visible already through the clouds of the last war in the characters of Joyce Cary, has to conclude, however reluctantly, on an admission of the deceptiveness of Gulley Jimson's solidity. In the art of the novel man can be reconfirmed only if his counterfeit character regains unequivocal solidity. This is the only way fiction can combat dissolution. However much one had wanted to believe that after this had been attempted by Stella, it had been achieved by Gulley, we finally must lay down our arms and admit our defeat. The story of the twentieth-century English novel so far seems to be that of a protracted dissolution of human personality with vain attempts at an integration that was not to be attained at the time this century moved into its latter half.

The metaphor of *The Picture of Dorian Gray* comes to mind. Oscar Wilde, who in his dilemma, resorted to escape, seems to have obliquely indicated a way back to reality. Shall we have enough fortitude to reject the half-truths, fascinated as we seem to be by the attractive fallacy of short cuts to salvation which our age keeps breeding in such quantities? Shall we find the courage to look into our own minds, admit the truth of the reflection of ourselves, however ugly and deformed it might appear? Or shall we stab it with indignation and so bar our way toward recovery that can come only through the painful process of a merciless self-recognition?

Notes

Introduction

1. André Glaz, *Hamlet or the Tragedy of Shakespeare*, reprint from *The American Imago*, Vol. 18, No. 2 (Summer, 1961), p. 131. The terms here used have been borrowed from a passage so important that I should like to quote them in context:

> The total potential that is available to an artist might, for convenience sake be visualized in terms of a scale extending from the material "realistic" world of the senses at one end, to fantasy, dreams and hallucinations at the other. A creative act is the result of the playing back and forth between the two. The created work of art, the fiction, is in the middle of the scale and draws its life from the "realistic" world on the one hand and from the world of fantasy on the other.
>
> In dramatic art the stage is the device, the fiction, the catalytic agent, so to speak, that vitalizes and coheres the raw stuff of both the real world and of fantasy. As material from the real world becomes actively engaged in the fiction of stage it moves toward fantasy. As dream material becomes engaged in the fiction it moves toward reality.

2. T. S. Eliot, *Selected Essays* (London: Faber and Faber, 1951), p. 25.

1 – Jim

1. Joseph Conrad, *Lord Jim* [1900] (The Modern Library, New York, 1931), p. 323 — hereafter cited as *Jim.*
2. *Ibid.*, p. IX; 3. *Ibid.*, p. IX; 4. *Ibid.*, p. 416.
5. *Ibid.*, p. IX; 6. *Ibid.*, p. 3; 7. *Ibid.*, p. 341.
8. *Ibid.*, p. 342; 9. *Ibid.*, p. 9; 10. *Ibid.*, p. 9.
11. *Ibid.*, p. 20.
12. Often mentioned. See pp. 43, 93, 106, 224, 325, 331, 361 and elsewhere.
13. *Jim*, p. 51; 14. *Ibid.*, p. 129.
15. *Ibid.*, pp. 44–45; 16. *Ibid.*, pp. 42–43.

17. *Ibid.*, p. 43; 18. *Ibid.*, p. 43; 19. *Ibid.*, p. 43.
20. *Ibid.*, p. 43; 21. *Ibid.*, p. 43; 22. *Ibid.*, p. 11.
23. *Ibid.*, p. 87; 24. *Ibid.*, p. 93.
25. *Ibid.*, p. 101; 26. *Ibid.*, p. 83.
27. William Shakespeare, *Macbeth*, Act V, Scene 1, line 56.
28. *Jim*, p. 325; 29. *Ibid.*, p. 80.
30. *Ibid.*, pp. 212–13; 31. *Ibid.*, pp. 214–15.
32. *Ibid.*, p. 324; 33. *Ibid.*, p. 247; 34. *Ibid.*, p. 385.
35. *Ibid.*, p. 335; 36. *Ibid.*, p. 318; 37. *Ibid.*, p. 246.
38. *Ibid.*, p. 384; 39. *Ibid.*, p. 386; 40. *Ibid.*, p. 387.
41. *Ibid.*, p. 384; 42. *Ibid.*, p. 394; 43. *Ibid.*, p. 408.
44. *Ibid.*, p. 408; 45. *Ibid.*, p. 409.
46. *Ibid.*, p. 409; 47. *Ibid.*, p. 409.
48. *Ibid.*, pp. 415–16.
49. *Ibid.*, p. 111; 50. *Ibid.*, p. 93.
51. William Shakespeare, *Hamlet*, Act III, Scene I, lines 83–88.
52. *Jim*, p. 102; 53. *Ibid.*, p. 95.
54. *Ibid.*, pp. 330–31; 55. *Ibid.*, p. 341.
56. *Ibid.*, p. 80; 57. *Ibid.*, p. 305; 58. *Ibid.*, p. 306.
59. *Ibid.*, p. 334; 60. *Ibid.*, p. 327.
61. *Ibid.*, p. 214; 62. *Ibid.*, p. 404.
63. *Hamlet*, Act V, Scene 2, lines 349–51.
64. *Jim*, p. 416; 65. *Ibid.*, p. 121; 66. *Ibid.*, p. 121.

2 – Ursula Brangwen

1. *The Letters of D. H. Lawrence*, edited and with an Introduction by Aldous Huxley (London: William Heinemann, 1934), p. 364 – hereafter cited as *Letters*.
2. D. H. Lawrence, "Morality and the Novel," *Phoenix, the Posthumous Papers of D. H. Lawrence* (New York: Viking, 1936), p. 527.
3. D. H. Lawrence, "Why the Novel Matters," *Phoenix*, p. 535.
4. D. H. Lawrence, *The Rainbow* [1915] (New York: The Modern Library, 1943), p. 203.
5. *Ibid.*, p. 345; 6. *Ibid.*, p. 200; 7. *Ibid.*, p. 207.
8. *Ibid.*, p. 205; 9. *Ibid.*, p. 206; 10. *Ibid.*, p. 203.
11. *Letters*, pp. XVII–XVIII; 12. *Ibid.*, p. 190.
13. *The Rainbow*, p. 215; 14. *Ibid.*, p. 248.
15. *Ibid.*, pp. 251–52; 16. *Ibid.*, p. 238.

17. *Ibid.*, p. 238; 18. *Ibid.*, pp. 242–43.

19. *Ibid.*, p. 244; 20. *Ibid.*, p. 263; 21. *Ibid.*, p. 408.

22. *Ibid.*, p. 406; 23. *Ibid.*, p. 407; 24. *Ibid.*, p. 407.

25. *Ibid.*, p. 413; 26. *Ibid.*, p. 419; 27. *Ibid.*, p. 466.

28. D. H. Lawrence, *Women in Love* [1920] (New York: The Modern Library, 1922), p. 8—hereafter cited as *Women in Love.*

29. *Ibid.*, p. 10; 30. *Ibid.*, p. 197; 31. *Ibid.*, p. 357.

32. *Letters*, p. 190; 33. *Ibid.*, p. 198.

34. D. H. Lawrence, "Preface to *The Grand Inquisitor*," *Selected Literary Criticism*, edited by Anthony Beal (London: William Heinemann, 1955), pp. 233–41.

35. See Isaiah Berlin, *The Hedgehog and the Fox* (New York: Simon & Schuster, 1953), pp. 67–71. Here is the text referred to:

> We—sentient creatures—are in part living in a world the constituents of which we can discover, classify and act upon by rational, scientific, deliberately planned methods; but in part (Tolstoy and Maistre, and many thinkers with them, say much the larger part) we are immersed and submerged in a medium that, precisely to the degree to which we inevitably take it for granted as part of ourselves, we do not and cannot observe as if from the outside; cannot identify, measure and seek to manipulate; cannot even be wholly aware of, inasmuch as it enters too intimately into all our experience, is itself too closely interwoven with all that we are and do to be lifted out of the flow (it *is* the flow) and observed with scientific detachment, as an object. It—the medium in which we are—determines our most permanent categories, our standards of truth, and falsehood, of reality and appearance, of the good and the bad, of the central and the peripheral, the subjective and the objective, of the beautiful and the ugly, of movement and rest, of past, present and future, of one and many; hence neither these, nor any other explicitly conceived categories or concepts can be applied to it—for it is itself but a vague name for the totality that includes these categories, these concepts, the ultimate framework, the basic presuppositions wherewith we function . . . "rational" and "irrational" are terms that themselves acquire their meaning and uses in relation to—"by growing out of"—it, and not *vice versa.* For what are the data of such understanding if not the ultimate soil, the framework, the atmosphere, the context, the medium . . . It is "there"—the framework, the foundation of everything, and the wise man alone has a sense of it.

36. See *The Rainbow,* pp. 413–14; 37. *Ibid.,* pp. 329–30.
38. *Ibid.,* p. 467; 39. *Ibid.,* pp. 434–35.

3—Stephen Dedalus

1. James Joyce, *A Portrait of the Artist as a Young Man* [1916] (New York: The Viking Press, 1956), p. 253—hereafter cited as *Portrait.*

2. James Joyce, *Stephen Hero* (London: Jonathan Cape, 1946), p. 17—hereafter cited as *Stephen Hero.* Here is the description:

> His [stiff] coarse brownish hair was combed high off his forehead but there was little order in its arrangement. [The face] A girl might or might not have called him handsome: the face was regular in feature and its pose was almost softened into [positive distinct] beauty by a small feminine mouth. In [the] a general survey of the face the eyes were not prominent: they were small light blue eyes which checked advances. They were quite fresh and fearless but in spite of this the face was to a certain extent the face of a debauchee.

3. *Portrait,* p. 17. The passage containing this image is a good example of how Stephen's interior life develops through a stream of associations that derive from repeated outward stimuli, in this case sensory, acoustical: "It was like a train going in and out of tunnels and that was like the noise of the boys eating in the refectory when you opened and closed the flaps of the ears. Term, vacation; tunnel, out; noise, stop. How far away it was! It was better to go to bed to sleep."

4. *Ibid.,* p. 247; 5. *Ibid.,* p. 246.

6. Stephen's rebellion would lend itself perfectly to psychoanalysis, but this would go beyond the scope of this essay.

7. When one gets acquainted with Conrad's early life in Poland, one seems to understand why the impression of a fatal futility of any revolutionary struggle had for ever impressed itself on Conrad's mind, just as it did much later on that of James Joyce. Different though the revolutionary rebels that used to meet at the deathbed of Conrad's father, their common property was that they were ineffectual, crushed as they were by the tzarist police. His parents' suffering in Siberia, his mother's death, his father's prolonged agony must have been too much for the growing boy coupled as they were by the shadows of heroes and traitors he caught flitting glimpses of in early childhood.

8. *Portrait*, p. 166; 9. *Ibid.*, p. 172.

10. "Medium" used in the sense as introduced by Isaiah Berlin in *The Hedgehog and the Fox*, see Ursula Brangwen, note 35.

11. *Ibid.*, p. 241; 12. *Stephen Hero*, pp. 26–27:
In spite of his surroundings Stephen continued his labours of research and all the more ardently since he imagined they had been 'put under ban.' It was part of that ineradicable egoism which he was afterwards to call redeemer that he conceived converging to him the deeds and thoughts of his microcosm.

13. Henry James, *The Art of the Novel* (New York: Scribner's Sons, 1947), p. 56—hereafter cited as *Art of the Novel*.

14. *Portrait*, p. 215.

15. *Ibid.*, p. 207; 16. *Jim*, p. 409.

17. *Portrait*, p. 238; 18. *Ibid.*, p. 247.

19. *Ibid.*, p. 253; 20. *Ibid.*, p. 159.

21. James Joyce, *Finnegans Wake* [1939] (London: Faber & Faber, 1949), p. 214—hereafter cited as *Finnegans Wake*. It is interesting to note that both passages quoted hereafter form part of the text James Joyce chose to read aloud and have recorded. It is peculiarly impressive when rendered in his voice with the local Irish accent.

22. James Joyce's *Ulysses* was published the same year as T. S. Eliot's *Waste Land*, 1922.

23. *Finnegans Wake*, p. 216; 24. *Ibid.*, p. 216.

4—Clarissa Dalloway

1. Virginia Woolf, *Mrs. Dalloway* (New York: Harcourt, Brace and Company, 1925), pp. 280–81.

2. *Ibid.*, p. 93; 3. *Ibid.*, p. 279; 4. *Ibid.*, p. 97.

5. *Ibid.*, p. 3; 6. *Ibid.*, p. 3; 7. *Ibid.*, p. 12.

8. *Ibid.*, p. 88; 9. *Ibid.*, p. 93; 10. *Ibid.*, p. 17.

11. *Ibid.*, p. 117; 12. *Ibid.*, p. 235; 13. *Ibid.*, p. 181.

14. *Ibid.*, p. 192; 15. *Ibid.*, p. 97; 16. *Ibid.*, p. 114.

17. *Ibid.*, p. 185; 18. *Ibid.*, p. 185; 19. *Ibid.*, p. 264.

20. *Ibid.*, p. 279; 21. *Ibid.*, p. 280; 22. *Ibid.*, p. 280.

23. *Ibid.*, p. 284; 24. *Ibid.*, p. 4.

25. *Ibid.*, p. 231; 26. *Ibid.*, p. 241.

27. *Ibid.*, pp. 231–32; 28. *Ibid.*, p. 254.

29. Lawrence Durrell, *Cefalu* (London: Editions Poetry, 1947), p. 62, very appropriately uses the word *Gleichgültig-*

keit, in the sense of acquired indifference in the case of another man who suffered from that kind of indifference as a consequence of war experience, this time in World War II.

30. *Mrs. Dalloway,* p. 135; 31. *Ibid.,* p. 137.

32. *Ibid.,* p. 139; 33. *Ibid.,* p. 281; 34. *Ibid.,* p. 281.

35. *Ibid.,* p. 282; 36. *Ibid.,* p. 244.

37. *Ibid.,* p. 293; 38. *Ibid.,* p. 280–81.

5—Tony Last

1. This is the epigraph for A *Handful of Dust* [1934]. Page references are to the Delta Book edition (New York, 1964).

2. *Ibid.,* p. 15; 3. *Ibid.,* p. 223.

4. *Ibid.,* pp. 77–78; 5. *Ibid.,* p. 101.

6. *Ibid.,* pp. 197–98; 7. *Ibid.,* p. 208.

8. *Ibid.,* p. 192; 9. See *Art of the Novel,* p. 56.

6—Major Scobie

1. Graham Greene, *The Heart of the Matter* [1948] (New York: Viking Press, 1965), p. 290—hereafter cited as *Heart of the Matter.*

2. *Ibid.,* p. 10; 3. *Ibid.,* p. 59; 4. *Ibid.,* p. 10.

5. *Ibid.,* p. 169; 6. *Ibid.,* p. 288; 7. *Ibid.,* pp. 6–7.

8. *Ibid.,* p. 5; 9. *Ibid.,* p. 149; 10. *Ibid.,* p. 149.

11. *Ibid.,* p. 32; 12. *Ibid.,* p. 55; 13. *Ibid.,* p. 142.

14. *Ibid.,* p. 128; 15. *Ibid.,* pp. 118–19.

16. *Ibid.,* pp. 282–83; 17. *Ibid.,* p. 27.

18. *Ibid.,* p. 128; 19. *Ibid.,* p. 253; 20. *Ibid.,* p. 84.

21. *Ibid.,* p. 129; 22. *Ibid.,* p. 125; 23. *Ibid.,* p. 127.

24. *Ibid.,* p. 52; 25. *Ibid.,* p. 192; 26. *Ibid.,* p. 44.

27. *Ibid.,* p. 44; 28. *Ibid.,* p. 280; 29. *Ibid.,* p. 253.

30. *Ibid.,* p. 253; 31. *Ibid.,* p. 288.

32. See Lydia's assessment of her first Polish husband, *Rainbow,* p. 244.

33. *Heart of the Matter,* p. 259; 34. *Ibid.,* p. 181.

35. See Aldous Huxley, Rampion, modelled on D. H. Lawrence, discussing St. Francis in *Point Counter Point* (New York: Harper Brothers, 1928), p. 399.

36. The motto of the novel is: "Le pecheur est au coeur même de chrétienté . . . Nul n'est aussi compétent que le pécheur en matière de chrétienté. Nul, si ce n'est le saint. Peguy."

37. *Heart of the Matter,* p. 141; 38. *Jim,* p. 416.

7 – Mrs. Jardine

1. Rosamond Lehmann, *The Ballad and the Source* (London: Collins, 1944), p. 101.
2. *Ibid.*, p. 27; 3. *Ibid.*, p. 10.
4. *Ibid.*, pp. 119–20; 5. *Ibid.*, p. 101.
6. *Ibid.*, p. 62; 7. *Ibid.*, p. 104; 8. *Ibid.*, p. 145.
9. *Ibid.*, p. 236; 10. *Ibid.*, p. 238; 11. *Ibid.*, p. 119.
12. *Ibid.*, p. 119; 13. *Ibid.*, p. 64.
14. *Portrait*, p. 172; 15. *Ballad and the Source*, p. 243.

8 – Stella Rodney

1. Elizabeth Bowen, *The Heat of the Day* (New York: Alfred A. Knopf, 1949), p. 147 – hereafter cited as *Heat of the Day*.
2. *Ibid.*, pp. 99–100.
3. Henry James, *The Portrait of a Lady* [1881] (The Modern Library, New York, 1909), pp. 287–88. The passage referred to goes:

> When you've lived as long as I you'll see that every human being has his shell and that you must take the shell into account. By the shell I mean the whole envelope of circumstances. There's no such thing as an isolated man or woman; we're each of us made up of some cluster of appurtenances. What shall we call our "self"? Where does it begin? Where does it end? It overflows into everything that belongs to us —and then it flows back again. I know a large part of myself is in the clothes I choose to wear. I've a great respect for *things!* One's self—for other people—is one's expression of one's self; and one's house, one's furniture, one's garments, the books one reads, the company one keeps—these things are expressive.

4. This really points to a loss of confidence in the power of human personality. The more diffused it seems to be, as though spreading over everything and everybody it gets in touch with, the less firmly fixed it is in any "still centre" of its own. Though containing an important grain of truth this is an early indication—like so many other clues offered by this susceptible visionary of the future—of the growing awareness of the radical limits of man's strength, the increasingly passive acceptance of life, which according to the rationalistic liberal tradition, man was supposed to be willing to govern for himself.

5. *Heat of the Day*, p. 23; 6. *Ibid.*, pp. 23–24.

7. *Ibid.*, p. 24.

8. *Ibid.*, p. 25. It is interesting to note that Elizabeth Bowen uses the same epithet for Stella's description as Virginia Woolf for Clarissa Dalloway. The sentence is almost identical: "She was not wholly admirable" in *Heat of the Day*, p. 25—"She was never wholly admirable" in *Mrs. Dalloway*, p. 282. This, together with the title, points to a kinship in spirit between the older and the younger author. Whether Elizabeth Bowen had undergone Virginia Woolf's influence cannot be gauged; even if Virginia Woolf's artistry had helped her to make her own literary technique more pliable she never allowed the latter's influence to penetrate into her work and deprive it of its originality and authenticity.

9. *Heat of the Day*, p. 147; 10. *Ibid.*, p. 90.

11. *Ibid.*, p. 257; 12. See *Clarissa Dalloway*, note 29.

13. *Heat of the Day*, p. 100; 14. *Ibid.*, p. 217.

15. *Ibid.*, p. 217; 16. *Ibid.*, p. 308; 17. *Ibid.*, p. 308.

18. *Ibid.*, p. 306; 19. *Ibid.*, p. 288; 20. *Ibid.*, p. 313.

21. *Ibid.*, p. 100; 22. *Ibid.*, p. 195; 23. *Ibid.*, p. 269.

24. A line by Russian poet Konstantin Balmont, *A Book of Russian Verse*, edited by C. M. Bowra (London: Macmillan, 1943), p. 89.

25. *Ibid.*, p. 100; 26. *Ibid.*, p. 147.

27. This is what I think Sartrean "mauvaise foi" really means. See Jean-Paul Sartre, *L'Être et le Néant* (Paris: Librairie Gallimard, 1943), pp. 85–111.

28. *Heat of the Day*, p. 233.

9—Gulley Jimson

1. Joyce Cary, *The Horse's Mouth* [1944] (London: Michael Joseph, 1946), p. 35—hereafter cited as *Horse's Mouth*.

2. *Ibid.*, p. 82.

3. *Herself Surprised* (1941), *To Be a Pilgrim* (1942), *The Horse's Mouth* (1944).

4. *Horse's Mouth*, p. 121; 5. *Ibid.*, p. 64.

6. *Ibid.*, pp. 54–55; 7. *Ibid.*, p. 55.

8. *Ibid.*, p. 58; 9. *Ibid.*, p. 14; 10. *Ibid.*, p. 220.

11. *Ibid.*, p. 290; 12. *Ibid.*, p. 35.

13. *Ibid.*, p. 42; 14. *Ibid.*, p. 291.

15. References to that effect run through the book, each time differently expressed, e.g., "THE OLD HORSE DOESN'T SPEAK ONLY HORSE," p. 44; "take a straight tip from the stable," p. 90; "straight from the stable," p. 282; "and that's real horse's meat," p. 291.

16. *Ibid.*, p. 286; 17. *Ibid.*, p. 286; 18. *Ibid.*, p. 286.

19. *Ibid.*, p. 286; 20. *Ibid.*, p. 286.

21. *Ibid.*, p. 286; 22. *Ibid.*, p. 180.

23. The trilogy with its cross references, each novel told by another of the three characters, holds a kind of mirror to reality, specially to the three characters concerned. It indicates that multiplicity of life's aspects and of the facets of human personality, just as it points to the relativity of human truth depending as it does on one's angle of vision.

24. *Horse's Mouth*, p. 91; 25. *Ibid.*, p. 210.

26. *Ibid.*, p. 210; 27. *Ibid.*, p. 213.

28. *Ibid.*, p. 291; 29. *Ibid.*, p. 291.

30. *Ibid.*, p. 291; 31. *Ibid.*, p. 35.

10 – Reprise

1. *Jim*, pp. 349–50; 2. *Ibid.*, p. 43.

3. *Ibid.*, p. 323.

4. That Conrad was shocked reading his *Heart of Darkness*, as some would have it, is quite probable in view of the fact that he was so immersed in his work that he could hardly bridge the gap between his "daylight" being – if we may resort to Lawrencian terminology, and his creative one. See J. I. M. Stewart, *Eight Modern Writers* (Oxford: Clarendon Press, 1963), p. 201.

5. *Jim*, p. 121; 6. *Portrait*, p. 246.

7. "Being" in the sense D. H. Lawrence would have used it.

8. H. G. Wells, *The History of Mr. Polly* (New York: Duffield and Company, 1910), p. 318.

9. *Mrs. Dalloway*, p. 12.

10. *Ibid.*, p. 16, the text runs: "Year in year out she wore that coat; she perspired."

11. *Ibid.*, p. 139; 12. *Heart of the Matter*, p. 290.

13. *Ibid.*, p. 128; 14. *Ibid.*, p. 299.

15. Joyce Cary, "Prefatory Essay," *Herself Surprised* (London: Michael Joseph, 1960), p. 8.

Index

Act of creation, 39
Aeschylus, 66
Ali (character): *The Heart of the Matter*, 91, 149
Alienation, 48
Andrew, John (character): *A Handful of Dust*, 71, 73, 78
Anna Karenina, xiv
Archetype, 98
Art: the function of, 43; definition, 47
Artist: his task, 38; definition, 43
Artistic creation, xvii; artistic objectivity, 39
Art of fiction, 124; art of the novel, 159*n*
Authors lives: the purpose of their presentation, xix
Autobiographical writing, xix

Ballad and the Source, The, 97, 98, 99, 161*n*
Balmont, Konstantin, 162*n*
Barbon, Harry (character): Nosy in *The Horse's Mouth*, 128, 130
Beal, Anthony, 157*n*
Beckett, Samuel, 71
Bennet, Arnold, xvii, 54
Berlin, Isaiah, 33, 157*n*, 158*n*
Between the Acts, 145
Birkin, Rupert (character): *The Rainbow*, 30–31, 32, 36
Blake, William, 126, 137
Bowen, Elizabeth, xviii, 112, 113, 114, 118, 150, 161*n*, 162*n*
Bradshaw, Dr. (character): *Mrs. Dalloway*, 62
Bradshaw, Sir William (character): *Mrs. Dalloway*, 67

Brangwen, Anna (character): *The Rainbow*, 21
Brangwen, Gudrum (character): *The Rainbow*, 26, 30
Brangwen, Tom (character): *The Rainbow*, 24
Brangwen, Ursula (character): *The Rainbow*, xviii; criticism of, 20–37; mentioned, 138, 139, 141, 142, 156*n*
Brangwen, Will (character): *The Rainbow*, 21, 22
Brideshead Revisited, 71
Brighton Rock, 82, 83

Captain Brown (character): *Lord Jim*, 5, 11, 12, 16
Cary, Joyce, xviii, 123, 124, 138, 151, 152, 153, 162*n*, 163*n*
Catholicism, 87
Cefalu, 159*n*
Character: drawing, xiii, xvi; forming, xiv; in fiction, xiv, xv, xx, 36, 99, 124
Cherry (character): *The Ballad and the Source*, 104, 105
Colonel Jardine. *See* Jardine, Harry
Compton-Burnett, Ivy, xvii
Conception of the novel, 19
Conrad, Joseph, xviii, 1, 2, 5, 6, 7, 8, 9, 13, 14, 16, 17, 18, 42, 45, 47, 83, 92, 94, 95, 138, 141, 155*n*, 158*n*, 163*n*
Cornelius (character): *Lord Jim*, 10, 14
Cranly (character): *A Portrait of the Artist as a Young Man*, 41, 44
Cronin, A. J., xvii

165